WHERE THE
HEART IS

WHERE THE HEART IS

Deborah & Anthony Hayward

ORION

CONTENTS

Many people have helped us in our research for this book. We would particularly like to thank the following: original writer and co-creator Ashley Pharoah; producers Kate Anthony and Avon Harpley; production secretary Lisa Buckley; production designers Alan Davies, Robert Scott and Paul Rowan; nursing adviser Margaret Tiffany; cast members Pam Ferris, Sarah Lancashire, Tony Haygarth, Jason Done, Marsha Thomason, Maggie Wells, William Travis, Kathryn Hunt, Laura Crossley, Andrew Knott, Melanie Kilburn, Neil McCaul, Alex Carter, Simon Ashley, Jessica Baglow, Graham Turner and Katrina Levon; programme publicist Naomi Phillipson; and Trevor Dolby and Pandora White at Orion Media. We should also like to thank Margaret and Ralph Tuck, and Danielle, Clare, Alexander and Olivia.

First published in 1999 by Orion Media
An imprint of Orion Books Ltd
Orion House, 5 Upper St Martin's Lane, London WC2H 9EA

A CIP catalogue record for this book is available
from the British Library.

ISBN 0-75281-819-8

Printed and bound in Italy by Printer Trento srl

FOREWORD

When ITV launched *Where the Heart Is*, the beautiful West Yorkshire landscape provided the perfect backdrop to a story about district nurses in a close-knit community. The programme was the result of a collaboration between writer Ashley Pharoah and script executive Vicky Featherstone, and its heartwarming overall feel enabled them to include some daring stories that might not otherwise have been acceptable for mid-evening viewing.

With Pam Ferris and Sarah Lancashire—both familiar faces to television audiences—in the starring roles of sisters-in-law Peggy Snow and Ruth Goddard, *Where the Heart Is* soon became compulsive Sunday evening entertainment for more than 12 million people. After three series, it remains a success story that looks set to run and run.

We hope this book serves as a reminder of some of the stories that have made the programme so popular, as well as providing an insight into the making of the series from the viewpoint of all those involved, including the actors who appear in it.

NURSING AN IDEA

THE CREATORS

After taking a postgraduate course at the National Film School in Beaconsfield, Buckinghamshire, Ashley Pharoah was nominated for a BAFTA award for his short film *Water's Edge*.

Commissions from the BBC followed, but these failed to reach the screen... until Ashley contacted the producers of *EastEnders* and ended up writing 30 episodes of the serial over three years. He particularly enjoyed scripting two hours' worth set in Clacton-on-Sea, Essex, where Pat, Ricky and David were searching for Frank. 'I had no storylines as such,' he recalls. 'It was just a chance to explore those characters. But that's what made my mind up to leave and find my own voice.'

Ashley was subsequently asked to write for *Casualty* and *Silent Witness*, and it was while working on the latter that he met Vicky Featherstone, who was the series' script editor.

A visit that Vicky made to the Colne Valley in 1995 gave Ashley the West Yorkshire setting and also the main characters of *Where the Heart Is*. Even though the story revolved around community nurses, he was adamant that—despite his previous screen credits—it was not going to be a medical drama.

'I love writing about medical matters, but I'm a bit squeamish in real life,' he admits. 'When we were researching *Silent Witness* we had to go to a mortuary to watch a post-mortem. That was horrific. I was pleased to get away from pathology to write *Where the Heart Is*.'

After two series, Ashley and Vicky both left the programme, although Ashley remains a consultant. Vicky returned to the stage, to work with the award-winning Paines Plough Theatre Company as artistic director.

RIGHT: *Writer Ashley Pharoah drew on his own upbringing in a close-knit community in Somerset to create* Where the Heart Is *with Vicky Featherstone, after she had met a group of district nurses in West Yorkshire.*

The original idea for a television series featuring two community nurses, their families and the people living and working around them in a West Yorkshire mill town grew out of the individual experiences of two people. With his childhood in Nailsea, Somerset, in mind, television writer Ashley Pharoah wanted to create a pro-gramme that would convey a genuine sense of community. Over and above that, he was keen to create a character who (like himself) broke away from this close-knit environment during his teens.

Ashley's character eventually materialized as Stephen Snow in the ITV Sunday, night series *Where the Heart Is*, made by

The character of Stephen Snow, originally acted by William Ash, grew out of Ashley Pharaoh's desire to write about a teenager breaking away from the only community he has ever known.

United Productions for Anglia Television Entertainment. Both the geographical setting for the programme and the idea of the story being centred around community nurses came from Vicky Featherstone, who had previously worked as script editor on the BBC drama series *Silent Witness*, featuring Amanda Burton as a forensic pathologist.

'I'd scripted the first series of *Silent Witness*,' Ashley explains, 'so Vicky knew I was interested in writing something about a small community, and specifically about a teenage boy moving out of it. After she'd left to join United, she took me out to lunch one day and we talked about it. Vicky's proposal was to combine the idea of a teenager leaving home with her own recent experience when she'd travelled up to Yorkshire to attend a wedding. She'd found a very tight-knit community there and also met some district nurses, and she felt there was a lot of warmth, humour and closeness in all that.

'I didn't know that part of the country, and when she mentioned a series about district nurses set in Yorkshire I really wasn't up for it. It wasn't what I was interested in doing—it sounded soft and sentimental. But she persuaded me to go up there with her on the train and meet these nurses, Margaret Tiffany in particular. We went to the little office in Meltham that they worked out of, where they made tea, took their phone calls and gossiped, and I immediately felt it was the kind of place that had valid stories to tell.

'Of course, I promptly asked them to tell me some of their stories, but they said they didn't have any. When we sat down, though, they soon began chatting away. One of their elderly patients had died that day and the nurses had tears in their eyes. They weren't devastated, but they were obviously moved. At that time I was living in London, and I knew that if I'd died in hospital there, there'd have been no tears at all because no one would even have known who I was.

'That was exactly what we were looking for—a sense of community. Not sentimentality, though, because there are bad things about small communities as well as good ones.

Community nurses Peggy Snow and Ruth Goddard (played by Pam Ferris and Sarah Lancashire) were to be the strong female characters at the centre of the action.

Everyone knows your business, for a start. But to someone living in a city that could seem quite attractive.

'We were there for two days and by the end of the trip I was completely sold on the idea and quite fired up. During that one visit I'd got all my characters together and nearly all the storylines for the first series, just based on things I'd been told or had experienced that weekend. It's the most painless writing job I've ever done.'

On his return from West Yorkshire, Ashley was commissioned by United's Controller of Drama, Simon Lewis, to write a script for a potential series. 'I wrote that first episode in isolation, without plotting out the other five,' recalls Ashley. 'We knew all along that it would be in a pre-watershed [before 9.00 pm] slot, so although I had to deal with some quite adult themes I couldn't include swearing or nudity.'

From this the two fictional community nurses Peggy Snow and Ruth Goddard emerged. Wanting a 'maternal heart' to the programme, Ashley based Peggy on his own mother, Maureen, who had died of cancer several years earlier.

'It wasn't her character exactly, but Peggy had the same qualities—quite modest ones of decency, warmth and down-to-earth humanity,' explains Ashley. 'I wanted that first series to be a tribute to my mother. Also, on a more pragmatic level, I needed someone to "drive" the stories every week. Peggy was a bit like an investigator. Some people might call that nosiness, but you need to have someone who's both caring and inquisitive. She had to be prepared to go under the surface of things to wheedle out the stories.

'As a foil for Peggy we wanted someone who was lively, younger, less experienced, and a little disrespectful. One of the nurses we saw in Yorkshire was a bit like that. That's how Ruth came about, and the comic *frisson* between her and Peggy was very attractive. There was also a lot of affection.

'To underline the sense of community, I thought it would be effective to make them related and introduce some tension into their friendship. As sisters-in-law they often get on well, but when they don't, family influences creep in. Again I was conscious that I didn't want it to be a sentimental pro-gramme, and from the start I tried to build in conflict. I wanted a bittersweet centre.'

At this stage no one had been cast in the lead roles, but the story was gaining a life of its own. 'I wanted to explore family life with the Peggy character,' Ashley recalls. 'I tried to write something relevant to viewers watching it as a family—no car chases, no guns. The big events in people's lives are often just small things like someone in the family moving away. Not earth-shattering, but a major event to the people involved.

'All the relationships just followed on from one another. There was the central dilemma of whether Stephen would go or not. Peggy, as his mother, would love him to stay but knows in her heart of hearts that he has to make his own way in the world. If Stephen didn't leave home, what would become of him? Although I loved his father, Vic, as a character, I was very aware that he wasn't a great success materially, and in his darker moments had regrets about the way his life had gone. At other times he appreciated that he had a fantastic family around him and was much loved. But if you never leave those tightly knit little groups, you always wonder "What if?". Stephen had seen that in his dad and there weren't going to be any "What ifs?" for him—he was going to get out there and check it out for himself.'

Seeing a toilet-paper factory in Meltham gave Ashley the idea of incorporating this into the story. 'The factory dominates the town in terms of employment,' he remarks. 'I thought it would be good to have that sense of industry. It gave us a workplace for the men that added a completely different angle from the women's nursing storylines.

'Also, I thought we might as well make the factory boss Ruth's husband, Simon. He's a Thatcherite but also part of a com-munity, which is quite an interesting para-dox. He's not a greedy man and takes a pride in providing jobs. Even though a lot of people don't much like him and even see him as ruthless and ambitious, without him they wouldn't have work.'

Ashley set the story in the fictional town of Skelthwaite, basing this name on the old mill town of Slaithwaite (pronounced 'Slough-it') where filming was to be centred. He made rugby the focal point for the men in the series. 'To balance the dark storylines, I knew we needed some comedy,' says Ashley. 'I'm rugby-mad myself and I liked the idea of a six-episode storyline about a crappy rugby team being turned into something presentable enough to beat their local rivals! I support Bath, who play Rugby Union, but I had to make it Rugby League in Yorkshire.'

The opening episode had a hard edge to it, with Peggy and Ruth acceding to an elderly cancer patient's wish to die by putting her on a commode when she was not fit to be moved. 'I was going to New Zealand and United wanted the first episode before I left, so I had to write it very quickly,' Ashley remembers. 'But I didn't want an episode where you simply introduce everybody, so I hit the ground running. In the very first episode the lead characters bumped off one of their patients! We were dealing with euthanasia in a family-viewing programme.

Comedy found its way into Where the Heart Is *with a rugby team that was determined to beat its local rivals.*

'Originally, I don't think the ITV Network Centre were exactly gagging for it. But I delivered the first draft and while I was out in New Zealand I got a phone call from Sue Hogg, who said that suddenly they were excited about it. They had a few concerns, though, and some rewriting was needed.

'Their biggest concern was to make sure the programme had a pyramid structure, with Peggy at the top. Rather than producing a "gang show", they wanted this matriarch to drive the narrative. They had to think about casting, and how to exploit the material commercially. One way was to get a well-known ITV actress, and this later turned out to be Pam Ferris. My rewrite, done in New Zealand, made things more explicit and gave her a more dominant role.'

United was commissioned to make six episodes of *Where the Heart Is*. Ashley, who arrived back from New Zealand in March 1997, then had to complete another five scripts before November of that year, when filming was due to start. Also, the production had to be got under way and all the characters had to be cast.

MARGARET'S INSPIRATION

Margaret Tiffany, who provided the biggest inspiration for *Where the Heart Is*, was a district nursing sister at Meltham Clinic in the Colne Valley.

Her son, John, knew theatre director Vicky Featherstone through working at the West Yorkshire Playhouse during the summer in the final year of his theatre studies degree course.

John invited Vicky, who by then was working as a script executive for United Productions, to his sister Rachael's wedding. She was overwhelmed by the narrow valleys, the closeness of the community and people's intense involvement in each other's lives, and thought it would make the ideal back-drop for a television series.

Lancashire-born Margaret and two of her colleagues subsequently helped writer Ashley Pharoah with his research for the first series of *Where the Heart Is*. Margaret also agreed to act as nursing adviser, providing information about various medical practices and answering all Pam Ferris and Sarah Lancashire's questions.

'District nurses are different from doctors,' emphasizes Margaret. 'We don't diagnose or prescribe—we identify symptoms and take them back to the doctor. On the other hand, we certainly can't be classed as just handmaidens to the doctor.

'I showed Pam and Sarah how to do bandages and dressings, and how to take blood pressure. I even had to demonstrate revival techniques by giving Graham Turner, the actor who plays Walter, mouth-to-mouth resuscitation. I also pointed out that district nurses always leave the patient's house exactly as they found it!'

In March 1997, shortly before *Where the Heart Is* was first seen on ITV, Margaret retired from her job as a district nursing sister after 23 years of working in the Colne Valley.

Pam Ferris and Ruth Lancashire were already known to ITV audiences when they were cast as Peggy Snow and Ruth Goddard.

CASTING THE NET

Kate Anthony was taken on as producer, although her previous experience had been in comedy, working on productions for the successful independent company Hat Trick. 'It was a big departure for me to go into drama,' Kate recalls. 'When I read the first script, I was incredibly moved by the story of a woman choosing to die in her own home, in a bleak farmhouse. Even after this one script I felt I knew all the main characters: Peggy, Ruth, Vic, Simon and Stephen.

'I went to West Yorkshire with Ashley and Vicky in the spring of 1996 and drove through Slaithwaite, Meltham, Marsden and the surrounding area, which we planned to use for the locations. Everything seemed to be coming to life, with the sun gleaming down and the moors looking so beautiful. Of course, when we started filming in the winter, the sun never came out again!'

After assigning three directors to the six episodes—two episodes each—Kate set about the task of finding actors to play the main characters, in collaboration with Simon Lewis and casting director Gail Stevens. Also consulted on the casting were Ashley Pharoah and Vicky Featherstone. 'Where the Heart Is wasn't intended as a vehicle for any particular actresses,' Kate explains. 'The starting point was the story, which came from Vicky and Ashley.

'The role of Peggy required someone who had tremendous innate strength and resolve, but at the same time an incredible warmth and humour, so that patients would feel re-assured. We wanted someone the audience would already know and be pleased to see, and came up with Pam Ferris.'

Remembered fondly for her television role as Ma Larkin in The Darling Buds of May, about a family living the life of Riley and not paying their taxes in the Kent of the 'fifties, Pam had since been offered, and rejected, many 'mumsy' roles similar to her character in that popular series. But she was keen to play community nurse Peggy Snow, who balances her career with family life within a close-knit West Yorkshire community.

'I read the first script and just loved it,' Pam enthuses. 'It was very daring, with a dark beginning about helping a woman to die. Ashley Pharoah, the writer, had the power to write about ordinary people, talk-ing about everyday things, then suddenly make something happen that would make you cry.'

The actress Sarah Lancashire, who had already announced her intention to leave Coronation Street after more than 600 episodes as dim-but-loveable Raquel Watts, was approached to play Peggy's sister-in-law, Ruth Goddard.

The actress was attracted by the fact that Where the Heart Is was not just a medical drama. 'It's about a small community of people whose lives are terribly ordinary,' she comments. 'Nothing outrageous is ever going to happen in Skelthwaite, but it isn't a mundane existence, either. There's also a great warmth and a strong community feel about the place. It seems to highlight the nicer aspects of life.'

According to producer Kate Anthony, Sarah was just as enthusiastic about the programme as she was herself: 'She'd read the script and, from that minute on, was keen to do it. She certainly didn't need any persuading. It was wonderful for us that someone like Sarah, who'd become a national icon in Coronation Street, came in and knew exactly what we were trying to do with Where the Heart Is, and was so excited about it.

'As with Peggy, in the character of Ruth we were looking for qualities of strength,' Kate adds, 'but her sense of humour is more cheeky and irreverent.'

Series creator Ashley Pharoah was unsure at first about two well-known personalities being cast in the lead roles. 'When they first came up with Pam and Sarah, I wasn't too keen,' he admits. 'I'd only ever written for the BBC and was very wary about ITV cast-ing Pam, as she was still so closely associated with The Darling Buds of May, and in Sarah's case taking someone straight out of a soap. It felt too constructed. But then they came to meet me separately—Simon Lewis, Vicky Featherstone and Sue Hogg— and I was completely knocked out. They were fantastic and all had very intelligent, sympathetic readings of the script. I was converted!'

Having cast the two female leads, around whom much of the action was to take place, finding the right actors to play their husbands proved a problem and many people were auditioned. 'It was really difficult,' recalls Kate Anthony, 'because the characters of

Ruth and Peggy were so strong.

'For Peggy's husband, Vic, for example, it would have been very easy to cast someone who didn't match Peggy's strength, which could have put everything out of balance. At the same time, he had to be someone you could believe was contented working for his brother-in-law in the paper factory and also loved rugby. We saw a lot of actors, but Tony Haygarth stood head and shoulders above everyone else. He had all the qualities of strength and humour—as well as the potential to be a bit grumpy at times.'

Thomas Craig was cast as Ruth's husband, Simon, only a few weeks before filming began, having originally auditioned for a smaller role in one of the first two episodes. 'He came in for another role,' Kate explains, 'saying that, whether he got the part or not, he'd got some fireworks from his mates and he could let us have them cheaply for Bonfire Night. That was *so* Simon! After Thomas had left, we talked about giving him the other role, but then suddenly I thought no, he's Simon.'

The role of teenager Stephen Snow was given to William Ash, who had trained at the celebrated Oldham Theatre Workshop as a child and was only just out of his teens himself. He was already known to television viewers as young squaddie Jack Stubbs in *Soldier Soldier*. Maggie Wells, whose television and theatre career went back to the 'seventies, was cast as part-time community nurse Patricia Illingworth.

Smaller parts went to William Travis (as factory worker Dick Lampard), Laura Crossley (as Stephen's sometime girlfriend, schoolgirl Deborah Alliss), Andrew Knott (as Stephen's sixth-form schoolfriend Henry, who gained the surname Green in the third series), Jessica Baglow (as Stephen's younger sister, Lucy) and Simon Ashley (as rugby player Terry).

As the programme began to be a success and went into further series, all of these characters became an important part of the Skelthwaite community.

Another member of that community, who would appear on and off, was Walter Charlton. Kate Anthony saw the potential to turn him into a character rather different from the one envisaged by Ashley Pharoah.

'Initially, Walter had been conceived as an old man in the vein of *Last of the Summer Wine*,' she recalls. 'We first interviewed Graham Turner for another role, but found he wasn't right for it. We liked him, though, and he really seemed to understand what we were trying to do with *Where the Heart Is*.

'Then I wondered about the character of Walter and thought perhaps it would be more challenging to make him a younger man with learning difficulties. His place in the community then becomes very clear-cut —he isn't really able to cope on his own, so he needs everyone around him for support.

'There are lots of older male characters in television dramas and comedies, often the village tramp or whatever, but you don't always know whether they're supposed to be suffering from Alzheimer's disease or just a bit forgetful and unable to do as much because they're old. I felt it was much braver to take on someone with a specific learning difficulty and show how he fitted into the community, rather than a comfortable, more familiar sort of figure.'

Walter was not based on anyone in particular, but Kate had experience of people with learning difficulties through being a social worker before entering television. 'I also have a brother with Down's syndrome,' she adds. 'That's a very different situation from Walter's, but perhaps it made me more keen to present the problems of a man with

learning difficulties living in the community. It was something I was more aware of, and I was determined to tackle the issue head on rather than fudging it.'

CREATING REALITY

Pam Ferris and Sarah Lancashire carried out a great deal of research in order to make their roles as believable as possible. 'We met Margaret Tiffany, who took us to the nursing practice in Meltham where she worked,' explains Pam. 'We weren't actually able to go out on visits with her, because that would have been unethical, but we were allowed to discuss their work.

'There are strict rules governing the limits of the nurses' responsibilities, but they break them all the time. For example, they often voluntarily pop round the corner and get someone a loaf of bread because the person can't get out, or make sure that someone gets a cup of tea in the morning.

'There are also rules about never touching a patient without rubber gloves on. And if you're applying any form of dressing, you always wear a plastic apron. But we discovered that, if you try to film it like that, first of all there's a lighting problem caused by the shininess of the apron, and secondly there's too much delay caused by putting it on. So we decided to take liberties with that sort of thing. I can understand if people complain about little points like that, but it *is* a drama, not a documentary.'

With all the research done and the scripts written, the cast and crew travelled to the Colne Valley area of West Yorkshire to make the first series of *Where the Heart Is...*

Thomas Craig (far left) and Tony Haygarth landed the roles of paper factory boss Simon Goddard and his brother-in-law, Vic Snow.

IN THE HEART OF THE COLNE VALLEY

A new television series was in the making —firmly located in the Colne Valley. This scenic area is home to several of West Yorkshire's old mill towns, whose nearest big centre is Huddersfield. Not far away is Holmfirth, used as the location for filming *The Last of the Summer Wine*, the comedy series based on the everyday adventures of a group of men in their twilight years. However, neither *Where the Heart Is* creators Ashley Pharoah and Vicky Featherstone nor producer Kate Anthony wanted their programme to exude that kind of quaint cosiness.

'When looking for specific locations in the spring of 1996, we were struck by the spectacular scenery around Slaithwaite and Meltham,' Kate recalls, 'but in the winter it can be very harsh. We saw the fictional town of Skelthwaite as a bit like a character itself, always beautiful but at times coming across as very cold. If it was your home and you were reliant on the local community, like Walter with his learning difficulties, Skelthwaite could appear as the most wonderful place to live. But if you were a teenager eager to move on, like Stephen, it could seem like the last place on Earth you'd want to be.

'Although we had such a stunning backdrop, we made a firm decision not to idealize it and make it chocolate-boxy. We didn't want Peggy living in a pretty little cottage by a brook, for example. The programme was very definitely set in Yorkshire, but we meant it to have a universal feel. We made Peggy's house the kind you could find in Devon, Scotland, London or anywhere else—even though her garden backed onto a moor stretching out into magnificent Yorkshire countryside.

'The same goes for the Health Centre. This was probably built in the 'sixties or 'seventies and is similar to ones you can find in Glasgow or Exeter, for example. And the school was just like the one I went to myself in Birmingham, except that it had a beautiful field behind it. We never wanted the characters to be country folk as such, but just ordinary townspeople, who don't wander around in green wellies with labradors.'

The Colne Valley offers stunning scenery but can be harsh in winter—the very combination that original producer Kate Anthony was looking for.

The Health Centre at Marsden provided a perfect setting for the one featured in Where the Heart Is.

With this brief, production designer Alan Davies and location manager Josh Dynevor set off into the area around Slaithwaite to locate all the regular settings for *Where the Heart Is*. When a second series was commissioned, Robert Scott—like Alan, a staff designer at Yorkshire Television—took over, and on the third series he was succeeded by freelance Paul Rowan. Both had to come up with new regular locations to add to those earmarked in the first place.

A real-life clinic that could double as Skelthwaite Health Centre was found in Marsden, a few miles west along the A62 from Slaithwaite. 'We looked at health centres over a wide area,' remarks Alan Davies, 'but most were tucked away in corners of places, and were either too small or not visual enough. At first we stayed away from Marsden because *Wokenwell* was being filmed there, but it certainly had the best health centre, which was in a lush green setting and had enough space for the cast and crew to work in.'

PAGES 24 & 25
The programme was to be set in Yorkshire, but with a universal feel.

There was one restriction, however: the clinic could be used for filming on Sundays only. So, with the increase to 14 episodes for the third series, the decision was made to continue filming exteriors there but to set up interiors in a studio at a former carpet warehouse in Milnsbridge—on the A62 in the other direction, between Slaithwaite and Huddersfield.

Bosses at the Meltham paper factory that Ashley Pharoah had spotted on his initial trip to West Yorkshire, when he first met Margaret Tiffany and the other real-life nurses, agreed to allow filming both inside and outside. This meant that the factory could play its part in the story as the home of Goddard's Paper Products, but again filming could only be done on Sundays. During the rest of the week it's business as usual for the

Filming at the real-life paper factory in Meltham that doubled as Goddard's Paper Products on screen was carried out at weekends so as not to disrupt the company's production schedule.

company, which buys paper in bulk for its production of toilet rolls and kitchen paper. Alan Davies was particularly impressed by the boss's office, as it has large windows looking down into the factory.

A location in which to film the interior and exterior of Peggy and Vic Snow's house was also found in Meltham. The living room, dining room, kitchen, hallway, staircase, three bedrooms and bathroom of the house were all used. The property's setting, with views of hills and stone walls behind, was favoured from the start by Herbert Wise, who directed the first two episodes of *Where the Heart Is*. However, designer Alan Davies was torn between this house and another one on the side of a hill above Slaithwaite.

'The biggest difficulty was that most houses in the area are tiny inside,' explains Alan. 'The advantage of the one we settled on was that it had a through lounge, with French windows and a patio with a view at one end, and bay windows looking out onto the street at the other. The problems were that there was only one door into the main room and the house was in a cul-de-sac, which could result in the film crew blocking residents in.'

For this reason, only exteriors have been filmed at the house since the beginning of the third series. Interior scenes have been filmed in the Milnsbridge studio where inside shots of the Health Centre are filmed.

'When we built the studio set we made the rooms slightly bigger, to give us more room for filming in,' reveals Paul Rowan. 'But it's not particularly noticeable on screen.

'The house is a busy one, with children—and it was even busier when Vic's sister and her family were staying in a caravan parked outside. So there's lots of clutter and washing around the place. Moving into a studio gave us more flexibility, and more time to film when we wanted to.'

24

SKELTHWAITE

Surrounded by hills and fields criss-crossed with stone walls, the fictional West Yorkshire mill town of Skelthwaite has a proud industrial past. It was once a local manufacturing centre, producing mostly textiles, but the mills have long been shut down and the factories now stand empty. The nearest big town is Huddersfield, but Leeds is the preferred destination for those looking for a night of clubbing.

Goddard's Paper Products is an example of modern-day industry in the town. Owned by Simon Goddard, it produces toilet rolls and kitchen paper for customers as far away as America.

General practitioners can be found at Skelthwaite Health Centre, which is also the base for the community nurses who make home visits to people throughout the district. Hospital patients have to travel to Huddersfield or beyond.

Old houses built of Yorkshire stone can be found in the town centre, but further out there are newer, brick buildings and two council estates. Shops include a small supermarket, an off-licence, a pharmacy, a florist and a hardware store. A curry house can be found in nearby Haleford, which is also home to the Lord Harris School for children with emotional and behavioural difficulties.

The Skelthwaite Arms is a popular local pub and the 'home' of the local rugby club, which used its basement as a changing room until money was raised to build a clubhouse next to its home ground. As the Skelthwaite Scorpions gradually lost players, they finally merged with their bitter rivals the Hoxton Giants, to become the Giant Scorpions.

The canal towpath has been used as a training run by the players, and there are both primary and high schools for the local children in Skelthwaite, which also has its own parish church and railway station.

With Simon Goddard owning the paper factory, it was only natural for him and wife Ruth to live in a more expensive home than his sister Peggy's. An ideal house for the Goddards was found on the hills outside Slaithwaite.

'It's a barn conversion—just the kind of place a man like that would have,' explains Alan Davies. 'There was clearly money there. It had good working space inside, the décor was much as we had envisaged, and the taste was quite nice and soft, which suited the character of Ruth. I just made the living room a bit heavier, to reflect Simon's character. We brought in a leather sofa and hard tables, and put some black into it.'

The rugby pitch used by the Skelthwaite Scorpions (who eventually amalgamated with their arch-rivals, the Hoxton Giants, to become the Giant Scorpions) is in the hills above Slaithwaite. In real life this is used by local team the Slaithwaite Saracens, who take part as extras in matches filmed for the programme. The clubhouse that was added at the end of the second series is, in fact, a three-sided shell with no interior.

The Skelthwaite Arms—the rugby club's base—is in reality The Silent Woman pub in Slaithwaite. 'It's quite big, which is always helpful,' says Alan Davies, 'and it has an L-shaped bar, which meant that we could shoot conversations across it diagonally. We also added quite a lot of rugby club memorabilia, such as trophies and cups, shirts and team photographs.

'In the story the rugby club's changing room was originally in the basement of the pub, but we actually filmed it in the basement of Slaithwaite Town Hall.'

Holmfirth High School has been used for scenes set in the fictional Skelthwaite High School, of which Stephen Snow, Deborah Alliss and Henry Green were pupils in the first

The Silent Woman pub in Slaithwaite becomes the Skelthwaite Arms during filming.

series. Stephen returned there as a classroom assistant for the third series, after his younger sister Lucy had moved up to the High School from Skelthwaite Junior School and Craig Harrison had started there on arriving from Bradford. Pupils of the real high school have been used as extras in some scenes for the programme, filmed there on Sundays. The junior school that was seen in the programme is, in reality, in Milnsbridge.

Several different hospitals in Leeds and the Huddersfield area have been used in *Where the Heart Is*, depending on the requirements of the script. For an interior scene of Walter Charlton in hospital during the first series, Alan Davies designed a set at Yorkshire Television's studios in Leeds.

For the third series several important new locations were added by Paul Rowan, who has substantial experience of working on period dramas. His credits include *The Grand*, *Wuthering Heights* and Granada Television's *Sherlock Holmes* series.

In the story, the newly arrived Harrison family purchased a cottage and adjoining barn to convert, so Paul found one that really had been bought for conversion by a couple, at Polegate Moor, high up in the hills above Slaithwaite. Both interiors and exteriors were filmed at this location, but the actors never looked forward to bearing the brunt of the weather, which, even when spring arrived, could be bitter.

'The place has spectacular views,' remarks Paul. 'The brief was that it had to be stunning but run-down, only not so bad that you couldn't tackle the conversion job. It had a roof on it and all the floors were safe. We saw the whole thing through as it was rebuilt, rewired and redecorated. But it won't be used for another series, because the locals who've bought it in real life are doing something completely different with it.'

One new location that may have a better chance of surviving is the rented house that Stephen Snow and his pregnant girlfriend Jacqui Richards moved into during the last part of the third series. Paul Rowan found a suitable small cottage in the hills near Meltham. 'It's actually someone's holiday cottage,' he explains, 'so we could just use it when we needed it and then put everything back as it was.

'I discovered the place as I was driving around the area and I thought it even looked like a rented house, which was just what we wanted. Because this was supposed to be Stephen and Jacqui's first home together, we were on the lookout for something that didn't look permanently lived in. It had a good feel to it in terms of furniture, so we simply added items such as cushions and throws to make it right for Stephen and Jacqui.'

Patricia Illingworth's house, seen for the first time in the second series, is actually located in Slaithwaite. 'We were looking for a small house that looked nice and homely —the kind a single woman would want to live in,' recalls production designer Robert Scott.

Similarly, Dick Lampard's flat had not been shown in the first series, so Robert had to locate somewhere that was suitable for a beer-drinking, rugby-playing bachelor. He found a three-storey block of flats in Milnsbridge for exterior filming and built an interior set in a church hall in the town.

The indoor set was switched to the Milnsbridge studio for the third series, which began with Dick's wedding to Cheryl.

'Originally the flat was untidy, with dirty washing everywhere and unwashed crockery in the sink,' says Paul Rowan, whose task it was to show the material changes in Dick's home life. 'But when Dick married Cheryl and she moved in with him, it became much more tidied-up. Suddenly there were flowery curtains instead of the blinds, and things like tablecloths, vases of flowers and houseplants appeared.'

Other locations that had to be found by Robert Scott for the second series included the Harrogate house where Ruth's grandmother Nell lived (in reality a red-brick Edwardian property in the Roundhay area of Leeds) and the Lord Harris School for children with educational and behavioural problems. Scenes at this establishment were shot at a similar real-life school near Chapel Allerton, on the outskirts of Leeds.

Venturing further afield, the residents of Skelthwaite have travelled to Scarborough, Whitby and the Lake District over the three series, which has given both cast and crew the opportunity to enjoy a break from their usual surroundings.

But all roads always lead back home to Skelthwaite.

GOING FOR A SONG

The theme song for *Where the Heart Is* was written and performed by Paddy McAloon, of pop group Prefab Sprout, whose biggest hit was the 1988 single 'The King of Rock 'n' Roll'.

'We wanted a song at the beginning,' explains original producer Kate Anthony, 'to tell people straight away that the programme was about home, family and community.

'Simon Lewis, the Executive Producer, remembered Paddy McAloon, who writes beautiful ballads, so I contacted his management company. As a result, I sent Paddy the script of the first episode and a letter saying we wanted the sort of song that would get Dad running in from the potting shed and Mum rushing from the washing-up in the kitchen—a song that was instantly recognizable and reassuring.

'Paddy read the script on Christmas Eve and loved it so much that he couldn't let it lie, so he got up on Christmas Day and wrote the song.'

Incidental music for the series is written by Tolga Kashif and Mark Sayer-Wade of The Music Sculptors, who had previously worked with original producer Kate Anthony.

PAM FERRIS
as Peggy Snow

When Pam Ferris took the starring role of community nurse Peggy Snow in *Where the Heart Is*, she was enthusiastic about playing a character that was much more like herself than either the earth-mother figure of Ma Larkin in *The Darling Buds of May* or the fearsome, child-hating headmistress Agatha Trunchbull in the film version of Roald Dahl's *Matilda*.

However, she found the quiet cosiness of the Kent countryside and the noisy glamour of Hollywood replaced by yet another set of experiences while filming this new series in the Colne Valley, near Huddersfield—where the weather can be very variable.

'On the first day's shooting, which started at 7.00am, I had to jog across a reservoir, and we ended up filming the scene eight times,' Pam remembers. 'It was a beautiful, bright November day, with not a cloud in the sky. By lunchtime on the second day, though, we had to stop filming because we were snowed up.'

But Pam felt that the changeable weather was a small price to pay for appearing in a programme which, in an intriguing way, tackled difficult issues within an outwardly comfortable community atmosphere.

'The character herself was very believable,' remarks Pam. 'Peggy had faults and wasn't a saint. She didn't come under the heading of "wonderful, wise woman" but made mistakes and came across as a whole, three-dimensional person.

'I liked Peggy's seriousness and commitment to her work. There are a lot of people like that around—women who have families and jobs, and juggle them quite successfully. I also found her relationship with her husband, Vic, very interesting. They'd become quite

tolerant in their old age but still had a bit of a romantic spark to them every now and again.'

Tony Haygarth, who plays Vic, had previously acted as Pam's husband in the 1989 children's comedy series *All Change*, alongside Frankie Howerd as an eccentric uncle. In this, they appeared as Northern chip-shop owners who swapped their lives with a well-off London couple. The experience helped the pair to step into the roles of man and wife on screen once again.

'We're both married to other people in real life,' explains Pam. 'There's a lovely, comfortable, easy way of behaving when you're married, and we both automatically slipped into that mode with each other. That's why I believe the relationship. It can take the odd tiff and still bounce back.

'From the start, I also loved Peggy's relationship with her son, Stephen. I liked her vulnerability—such as when he was starting to become interested in girls and she owned up to him very honestly that she wanted to be the only woman in his life. I found that very touching.'

With a screen daughter, too, Pam found herself playing mum to a family very different from the one that had made her a household name in *The Darling Buds of May*, based on the H E Bates books.

In that series, which also featured David Jason, Pam played the expansive Ma Larkin, serving up tasty, hearty meals for her happy-go-lucky farm family in the Kent countryside of the 'fifties. The programme became the first big new TV success of the 'nineties, but Pam had no idea it would become quite so popular and run for three series.

'I didn't think it was going to be earth-shattering,' she says. 'None of us realized it would be so "mega". But I have a theory that the programme's extreme Englishness and nostalgic quality were probably responsible for that.

'The country had just been through the terrible Gulf War, Margaret Thatcher was no longer prime minister, and we all felt a little rudderless. That's not to say she was a good leader, but she was strong. When *The Darling Buds of May* came along on a Sunday evening, it gave everybody emotional balm.'

Pam's own father worked for the Ministry of Defence and was stationed in Hanover, Germany, at the time she was born. When she was six the family moved to Wales, but they emigrated to New Zealand seven years later. On leaving school, Pam went into the rag trade as a pattern cutter and designer, and she enjoyed acting in amateur dramatics before making her radio début at the age of 17. After experience in the theatre in Christchurch and Auckland, she returned to Britain, anticipating being 'a small fish in a big pond'.

Acting and choreography work followed in repertory theatre in Ipswich, but then despondency began to set in—until Pam was inspired by seeing Judi Dench in *London Assurance* on the West End stage. Her first screen role came in director Mike Leigh's film *Meantime*, in which she acted a cockney mother with two unemployed sons (one of them played by Tim Roth). Pam then played the role of Stephanie Beacham's stepsister, Nesta, in the 'eighties television series *Connie*, set in the cut-throat world of fashion.

Ma Larkin was Pam's next big role, but she has also won admiration for playing a number of other classic parts on television, such as Mrs Dollop in *Middlemarch*, Eleanor in *The Rector's Wife*, Mrs Markham in *The Tenant of Wildfell Hall* and Mrs Boffin in *Our Mutual Friend*.

Pam was surprised by the enduring popularity among children—thanks to the wonders of the video age—of Miss Trunchbull in the film of *Matilda*, on which she worked alongside American actor Danny DeVito, who was also the film's director: 'I didn't know it would turn out to "have legs", as they say,' comments Pam. 'What Danny set out to do was to make a classic, and I think he succeeded.'

In the film Pam even performed her own stunts, which included jumping over a three-foot-high bannister onto a platform 15 feet below and swinging a girl round in mid-air. 'I trained with Olympic champion Bill Green,' she confides. 'As well as doing a circuit of weight machines every day, I learned the shot-put, hammer-throwing and javelin.'

Filming 12 hours a day for 125 days over six months proved gruelling, especially in temperatures of up to 120 degrees Fahrenheit. The heat even caused Pam to pass out at one point, and she was left with scars on her hands from holding the wires that helped to suspend the girl in mid-air.

Reflecting on the eccentric characters she has portrayed in the past, such as Ma Larkin and Agatha Trunchbull, Pam—who lives in London with her actor husband Roger Frost—remarks: 'Of all the parts I've ever played, Peggy in *Where the Heart Is* is the least extreme. She's the most naturalistic and the least divergent from myself.'

SARAH LANCASHIRE
as Ruth Goddard

After creating one of television's most cherished characters, dizzy barmaid Raquel Watts in *Coronation Street*, Sarah Lancashire stepped straight into the shoes of community nurse Ruth Goddard in *Where the Heart Is*—starting filming just two weeks after walking away from Britain's most famous cobblestones.

'Ruth is quite a strong character,' says Sarah. 'She's single-minded and very independent. I liked the fact that she's a working mum. She juggles everything, she's up with the baby, she's out to work, she sticks tea on the table—she does the lot, which is incredibly normal.

'During the first series Ruth was seen mostly with Peggy—they were always visiting patients together. Then, I think, people realized that the NHS didn't actually have the resources to continue sending community nurses out in twos, so we both did our home visits individually after that!

'But you're always working within certain parameters. There are some boundaries you can never cross in *Where the Heart Is*. If you're asking me whether I find that realistic, of course it's not realistic. But we're here to make a drama, not a fly-on-the-wall documentary.'

The drama of Ruth miscarrying and splitting up with husband Simon was welcomed by Sarah and actor Thomas Craig. 'There are only so many leg ulcers you can tend before you realize you aren't gaining enough job satisfaction,' says Sarah with a wry smile. 'The producers know you can't keep going out and doing that, so they take the character down a different avenue.

'So much of Ruth and Simon's relationship was taken for granted in the first two series that their domestic life was never really explored. But that all changed in the third series and Tom and I had far more to do together on screen. We had more dramatic scenes and were able to build up a relationship. That came as a breath of fresh air.'

One aspect of Ruth's life that was explored in the second series came when she was reunited with her grandmother, Nell, and it was revealed that her mother had emigrated to Australia after remarrying.

Sarah, who is divorced from composer Gary Hargreaves and lives in Cheshire with her two sons, Thomas and Matthew, is the daughter of television scriptwriter Geoffrey Lancashire, who wrote 74 episodes of *Coronation Street* over seven years, as well as working on Granada Television situation comedies such as *The Lovers*, *The Cuckoo Waltz* and *Foxy Lady*. Her mother also worked for Granada Television before leaving to become her husband's secretary while bringing up Sarah and her three brothers—her twin, Simon, elder brother John and younger brother James.

'My upbringing was an academic one,' explains Sarah, who attended Oldham Grammar School, where she passed eight O-levels and three A-levels. 'The fact that I've worked within the industry is no surprise to me after having two parents who've done so. The only difference was that I chose to go in front of the camera rather than behind it.

'After I'd finished my school education I explored the possibility of acting rather than production because I was very comfortable at a performance level. Fortunately, as soon as I came out of drama school I found work. If that hadn't happened, I might well have

side-stepped into production, and would have been more than happy to do so. It was the creative nature of the industry that attracted me to it.'

Performing in the Stephen Sondheim musical *Pacific Overtures* at the Library Theatre, Manchester was Sarah's first professional job. In between stage roles and small parts on television, she also taught drama at Salford University for four years, stopping only after landing the role of Linda in the West End production of *Blood Brothers*, alongside Kiki Dee.

Fame came in 1991 when *Coronation Street* offered Sarah the role of Raquel Wolstenhulme, the scatterbrained supermarket shelf-filler who became a barmaid at the Rovers Return and married Curly Watts, after having her heart broken both by a two-timing footballer and by Des Barnes. Sarah had, in fact, already appeared in the *Street* in 1987, as nurse Wendy Farmer who answered the Duckworths' advertisement for a lodger, but Vera thought she might be too much for Jack's blood pressure.

Raquel quickly became a firm favourite with viewers, but Sarah decided to leave the character behind after five years and some 600 episodes. She was thrilled that the audience took to Raquel but, a few years on, she has no desire to look back. 'I think it's about time people started to move on,' she remarks, 'and I have.'

In addition to joining *Where the Heart Is* after leaving *Coronation Street*, Sarah broke new ground by starring as pregnant Radio York news journalist Liz in a situation comedy, playwright John Godber's *Bloomin' Marvellous*, alongside former *Casualty* star Clive Mantle in the role of her husband, Jack. 'The BBC commissioned a second series, but I didn't want to do it,' explains Sarah. 'In any case, after one series, the journey was over—it was about a nine-month pregnancy.' In between series of *Where the Heart Is* Sarah has fitted in television roles in *Murder Most Horrid* and in *Verdict*, in which she played a barrister. She has also recorded a number of radio plays.

Now, the future of Ruth Goddard in Skelthwaite is uncertain, following her miscarriage, separation from husband Simon and decision to visit her mother in Australia. 'Ruth became very isolated,' observes Sarah. 'There was something missing in her life and she wanted to explore a world beyond Skelthwaite, which she was finding quite parochial and a bit suffocating. Also, she was now the same age as her mum was when she went to Australia and there were still a lot of questions that hadn't been answered, so she needed to meet her mother.'

1996–7

On Sunday 6 April 1997, at 8.00pm, the first episode of *Where the Heart Is* went out on ITV screens. Despite being heralded by newspaper critics as 'heartwarming', 'soft-centred' and 'a series which sets out unashamedly to warm the cockles of your heart', it had featured both a birth and a death before the first commercial break. The programme immediately attracted 12 million viewers, which it held on to throughout the six-part series—severely denting the ratings for the BBC series *Hamish Macbeth*. In fact, *Where the Heart Is* proved to be the most popular new television drama series of 1997.

The stories were set in the winter of 1996–7, between November and March, the period during which filming took place. As well as the events in the lives of the nurses' patients, the series featured the birth of Ruth and Simon's son, Alfie, and his subsequent abduction, teenager Stephen Snow's affair with his schoolteacher, the varying fortunes of the Skelthwaite Scorpions rugby club, and life at the town's paper factory.

In a change of scene for Episode 4, the nurses travelled to a conference in Scarborough, where Peggy was due to give a speech. In reality, those scenes were filmed in three different places: the East Coast seaside town itself, a hotel in Harrogate and the former Leeds Playhouse theatre, which was used for the sequence set inside the conference hall. In the story, the flustered Peggy abandoned her script and told the gathered crowd about her own mother's illness.

'It was very personal to Ashley Pharoah because it related to his own mother's death, which he transposed to Peggy's mother,' says Pam Ferris. 'It allowed me that long, seven-page speech, which I felt very privileged to make. It was a beautiful piece

Peggy Snow, husband Vic and children Lucy and Stephen had lived in Skelthwaite all their lives.

Ruth Goddard and husband Simon celebrated the birth of son Alfie in Episode 1 of the first series.

of writing and the process of shooting that scene linked me into the character of Peggy more than anything else. That's still there. She just has that tremendous compassion for people who are suffering and I find that very touching.'

But even Pam was taken aback by the success of the first series. 'I was quite shocked, but pleasantly surprised,' she admits, 'especially as I'd been told we'd be lucky to get eight or nine million viewers. In fact we attracted 12 million, and the beauty of it all was that we kept them. I was really thrilled, even though I'm not driven by ratings. My main pleasure in the work is being on the set and, if I can bear to watch it at a later date, not being too horrified with the result.'

Ashley Pharoah, on the other hand, who wrote all six scripts for the series, was prepared for the acclaim. 'I went to see the programme being filmed just before Christmas 1996, after having my head down in my office writing,' he recalls, 'and the atmosphere was fantastic. You could see that people were excited. Technicians came up to me and told me how good they thought it was, and that had never happened to me before. There was definitely a feeling that we'd pulled off something a bit special.'

However, on the first day of filming producer Kate Anthony wondered what she had let herself in for. 'It was my first drama, we were shooting at a farmhouse up in the hills above Slaithwaite and it had started to snow,' she remembers. 'It snowed so heavily that, as I stood at the farmhouse, I could see our vehicles, generator and props truck slipping down the lane as they were trying to come up. Our location manager, Josh Dynevor, contacted everyone in the area with a four-wheel-drive, and we had farmers and other locals coming out of nowhere. After two hours, the snow turned into a blizzard and we had to abandon filming. I wondered what on earth we'd been thinking of—filming in Yorkshire in the middle of winter!'

Despite this bad start, shooting schedules were largely adhered to and Kate soon began to feel more confident that everything was working out. 'Margaret Tiffany, our nursing adviser, really tapped into it,' says Kate. 'There are community nurses working in an urban environment who do a very different job from the one Peggy and Ruth do. They're incredible technicians these days, with a high level of training and terrific skills. But we were portraying a specific district nurse who worked in the area she'd been born and brought up in. Where does being a super-efficient nurse stop and being a good member of the community begin? *Where the Heart Is* was about this dilemma.

'Whereas many community nurses would say they'd love to sit down and have a cup of tea with their clients but just don't have the time, Margaret was saying she'd always stop for tea and a chat, even if it meant getting home late at the end of the day or missing out on her lunch break. But then, she might have been at school with the patient's daughter, or his wife might have been a friend of her mother's. Her job was to be there for the whole family, not just the patient. Once we all tapped into that, everything fitted into place.

'The day after the first episode was broadcast, we received the overnight viewing figures and I ran up and down the corridor practically doing cartwheels!'

PEGGY LANDS IN TROUBLE

- Martin Hutton, the prodigal son of elderly cancer victim Madeleine, was played by ANDREW READMAN, who is best known on television for acting policemen—DC Cannon, who arrested Steve McDonald in *Coronation Street*, and Inspector Mike Willis in *City Central*. He was also in the live-action film of *101 Dalmations*.

Nursing manager Elaine Trafford, who took Peggy Snow's statement after Martin's complaint, was played by MARJI CAMPI, who is remembered as Joyce Watson in the sitcom *Surgical Spirit*. She has also portrayed Jack Duckworth's fancy woman, Dulcie Froggatt, in *Coronation Street* and both Betty Hunt and Jessie Shadwick in *Brookside*.

On a bitterly cold winter morning, the rugged hills above Skelthwaite glowed white in the sunlight as two district nurses, sisters-in-law Peggy Snow and Ruth Goddard, drove over the ice to visit Madeleine Hutton on their first call of the day.

Madeleine was dying from cancer and in great pain. Her GP, Dr Underwood, felt that she should be in hospital, but the sick woman was adamant that she wanted to remain at home. Peggy and heavily pregnant Ruth both realized that their patient was hanging on to life in the hope of being able able to say a final goodbye to her estranged son, Martin, to whom she had not spoken for many years.

As the two nurses carried out their duties, bedbathing Mrs Hutton and making her comfortable, her husband, John, implored them to put his wife out of her misery. Peggy, knowing the unbearable agony Madeleine was in, decided to sit her on the commode, aware that any movement could kill her.

They then tucked her back into bed, where she died moments later. Just as the nurses were leaving, Martin arrived. He was devastated to discover that he had missed his mother by only a few seconds.

The long-lost son's arrival was met with anger on the part of his father and the two locked horns in a bitter row. With tempers running high, John unintentionally landed Peggy in the mire by telling Martin how she had not been prepared to let his mother go on suffering.

Martin saw red. He raced to Skelthwaite Health Centre, accused Peggy of murdering his mother and threatened to 'take things further'. At first, the nurse did not fully appreciate the gravity of her predicament, insisting that she had done the right thing, but the penny finally dropped when she was interviewed about the incident by nursing manager Elaine Trafford, who warned her that she could face murder charges.

Peggy attempted to reason with Martin and invited him to visit a hospice with her so that he could witness at first hand others suffering as his mother had. She hoped to get through to him by making him understand how much pain his mother had had to endure. Martin went along but appeared to be unmoved and resolved to continue with his accusation.

During a celebration at the Skelthwaite Arms, Peggy told Vic of the possible charges she faced and spoke of her growing fears that she could lose her job. Events then took a dramatic turn when Martin arrived at the pub after an emotional reconciliation with his father. He sought Peggy out and told her of his troubled history with his parents since the death of his sister, Sarah, in a car crash.

After falling out with Madeleine and John at Sarah's funeral, Martin had returned to London and none of them had spoken since. Martin said that he had tried to patch things up, but the final straw for him had been when his parents ignored an invitation to his graduation ceremony. There was hurt and anger on both sides, he admitted. After conceding that he had no right to be angry with Peggy, he said that he was withdrawing his allegations and the matter was closed.

TO RUTH A SON!

Simon Goddard was as proud as Punch when wife Ruth gave birth to baby Alfie six weeks early, after a dramatic dash to St Mary's Hospital, Huddersfield.

Returning from the visit to the Huttons' farmhouse, Peggy moved quickly into action as the pregnant Ruth went into premature labour. After a frantic dash to St Mary's Hospital in Huddersfield, Alfie was born—six weeks early but nevertheless weighing in at a healthy 6½ lb.

Skelthwaite's tiny newcomer was welcomed into the world by his proud-as-punch dad, Simon, who remained at Ruth's side throughout the birth. Simon was totally captivated with his young son, and remained happy just to gaze in wonder at him, until Ruth persuaded him to go down to the pub to celebrate.

LIKE FATHER, LIKE SON

● Epileptic schoolboy Billy Bevan's teacher, Mrs Shelley, was played by JO WARNE, the actress who originally took the part of Peggy Mitchell in *EastEnders* in 1991, when she chased to Gretna Green in a failed attempt to stop daughter Sam marrying Ricky Butcher.

SIOBHAN FINNERAN, who played Josie Phillips in *Coronation Street* and barmaid Heather Hutchinson in *Emmerdale*, acted the part of Billy's mother, Carol. In real life she is married to *Heartbeat* star Mark Jordon.

Peggy was called to Skelthwaite Junior School when her daughter Lucy's schoolfriend, seven-year-old Billy Bevan, was hurt in a playground accident. While treating his wounds, Peggy was shocked to find extensive bruising on the small boy's body and tactfully asked his mother, Carol, about this.

Peggy felt awkward when Carol took offence at her questioning and the headteacher, who labelled Billy as a child with severe behavioural problems, informed her that she intended to bring in the local social services.

But Peggy managed to delay this action while she looked into Billy's case—she was convinced that there must be a reasonable explanation for his behaviour and for the bruising. After all, she knew that Carol was a good mother who would never hurt her son.

So, after bumping into the boy and his mother while shopping, she invited Billy to join Lucy in accompanying her on her rounds. Billy was keen to go, and Carol and husband Joe spent the afternoon at home together.

The couple lay in bed discussing Billy—all he needed was love and understanding, said Joe, who did not want Billy to end up in a special school, as he had. He confided in Carol that he had been made fun of as a child and cruelly called 'Spaz Man' and 'Loony'.

Out on Peggy's rounds, things were going smoothly until Billy injured Lucy by pushing her from the haystack on which they were both sitting while Peggy and her colleague, Patricia Illingworth, helped a female patient who was stuck fast in an old tin bath.

Peggy, extremely concerned by Billy's actions, drove him straight home and told Carol that she, too, thought he had behavioural problems and should see a child psychologist. Carol, not keen but realizing she had no choice, agreed.

It was not all smiles when Peggy took daughter Lucy (Jessica Baglow) and schoolfriend Billy Bevan (Matthew Lewis) on her rounds.

While the two women were talking, Joe's worst fears were confirmed as Billy described the incident with Lucy to him. When the boy said that he could only remember dreaming, and then waking up to find someone shaking him and Lucy on the floor, Joe realized that Billy had the epilepsy from which he also suffered but had, until now, kept quiet about. Upset and angry, Joe threw Peggy out of the house and told her to mind her own business.

Arguing afterwards with Carol, Joe declared that he would rather move away to Leeds than risk having his son taken away from him. He stormed out and went to the Skelthwaite Arms. When he was later found on the ground outside the pub, having collapsed in a pool of his own vomit, everyone assumed he had been blind drunk. Back at home, Joe cleaned himself up and tearfully told Carol about his epilepsy.

Alarm bells rang for Peggy when Lucy confided in her that Billy had pulled faces before falling down and later did not remember anything about the incident. The experienced district nurse began to piece Joe's collapse and the information about Billy together. She then decided to go back to the Bevan house, where she discovered Billy having a fit on the hall floor while his parents rowed in another room.

An ambulance was called and Peggy allayed Joe's fears by assuring him that things were different these days—epileptics could now lead a normal life with the help of medication. Joe thanked her, after all, for 'sticking her nose in'.

TEACHER'S PET

It was a difficult time for Peggy's 18-year-old son, Stephen, who had to make important decisions about his future. His uncle, Simon Goddard, had offered him a job in his toilet-paper factory if he wanted to leave school and drop his ambitions of winning a place at university. Peggy and Vic breathed a sigh of relief when he decided to turn down the offer and continue with his studies.

When Stephen fell for young English and drama teacher Wendy Atkins (Susannah Wise), his mother threatened to report her unless she quit her job and left town immediately.

But Stephen's mother soon began to wonder what his studies were leading to. She was rather amused when she discovered a tiny white bra in her bed. 'It's like a doll's hammock,' she remarked to Ruth with a chuckle, having assumed that the garment belonged to Stephen's girlfriend, Deborah.

Peggy decided to hold her fire on the matter and to say nothing about it while her son was heavily involved in his school's production of the Tennessee Williams play *A Streetcar Named Desire*.

However, an even bigger surprise than the stray bra lay in store for Peggy when she returned home earlier than expected to find Stephen

in her bed with his young English and drama teacher, Wendy Atkins—just three years his senior. Peggy was shocked but managed to slip away to gather her thoughts, without disturbing the pair.

DAD CATCHES SUSANNAH IN BED!

● In her role as schoolteacher Wendy Atkins, SUSANNAH WISE found herself caught in bed with actor William Ash (as sixth-former Stephen Snow) by her father, Herbert Wise. But he didn't mind—he was the director!

'My first scene for *Where the Heart Is* was a bedroom scene with an actor I'd never met before, and Dad was directing,' recalls Susannah, who was already known to television viewers as Michaela 'Mick' Lennox in the hospital drama *Staying Alive*. 'I was so nervous about the scene that I forgot to be nervous about Dad,' she adds.

'We tried to keep things as professional as possible and I tried not to call him Dad in front of the rest of the cast. But I slipped up one time and brought the whole set of about 200 people to a standstill!'

Herbert, who directed the first two episodes of *Where the Heart Is* and helped to shape the series, has made hundreds of television programmes, including classics such as *I Claudius* and *Julius Caesar*.

Because it is so precarious a profession, he did not encourage Susannah to go into acting, and he had no involvement in her casting in *Where the Heart Is*. 'The producer happened to see Susannah in *Staying Alive* and asked if she could come in for an audition,' Herbert explains. 'I left it up to them as I didn't want to get involved.'

Susannah has also been seen on television in *The Ruth Rendell Mysteries: The Strawberry Tree*, *Class Act*, *Bliss*, *Casualty*, *The Bill*, *Dalziel and Pascoe*, *Faith in the Future* and *The Tenant of Wildfell Hall*.

She decided to confront Wendy at her home, where she threatened to expose her if she did not resign from her teaching post and leave Skelthwaite. Peggy was determined, and Wendy's professions of her love for Stephen only riled her even more.

At the party after the school play, Wendy informed Stephen that she could no longer go on seeing him. Ruth inadvertently overheard this conversation and felt sympathy for Wendy and Stephen. As Wendy walked home afterwards, Ruth tagged along, pushing baby Alfie in his pram, and explained that Peggy was so angry only because she adored her son. Wendy told Ruth that she did, too, but that she realized Stephen would eventually outgrow her.

Later that night, Stephen paid his teacher a visit. Unwilling to accept her rejection, he played on what he instinctively knew were Wendy's true feelings. She was unable to resist her young lover and the couple ended up in bed once again. Afterwards, in a final attempt to end their relationship, Wendy tried to be cruel to be kind, claiming untruthfully that she did not really love him.

Carrying out Peggy's wishes, she resigned from her job. Stephen was devastated when this news was delivered by the school's headteacher during morning assembly. He could not understand why Wendy had not told him herself about her apparently ill mother, and marched angrily into the classroom where she was teaching to demand that she meet him that evening.

Stephen clung on to the doomed relationship and was beside himself when Wendy, although finally confessing her feelings for him, said that she was still leaving Skelthwaite to be closer to her sick mother in London. Wendy's departure left Stephen brokenhearted and unable to accept that the relationship had really ended.

A MOTHER'S WORST NIGHTMARE

When Peggy Snow helped Gwen Phillips to move into St Margaret's Nursing Home, she had no idea of the chain of events about to be triggered. Peggy and Gwen's daughter Jean were called back when the old lady scalded her knee with a hot cup of tea, having recognized one of the other female residents, Martha Travis.

Peggy arrived with Ruth, who was still officially on maternity leave, and baby Alfie. While Peggy treated Gwen's knee, Alfie became a star attraction with the residents, who were all keen to have a cuddle. Obviously distressed, Gwen begged Jean to take her home. She refused to tell Peggy what was wrong and duly left with her daughter.

Distracted by Walter Charlton, a local man with learning difficulties, coming downstairs minus his trousers, Ruth momentarily lost track of Alfie and failed to notice Martha Travis leave with the baby in her arms.

A frantic search of the home was made, but Ruth became increasingly distraught as the seconds ticked by. On learning that Martha, who had been behaving strangely that morning, was also gone, Ruth insisted that the police be called in and her husband Simon contacted.

RIGHT: *Nursing home resident Martha Travis (Pauline Jefferson) grabbed baby Alfie Goddard and headed across the moors towards the village of her childhood—but it had gone and in its place stood a reservoir.*

Ruth and Simon went through hours of agony as police searched for Martha and their son, Alfie, with night falling and the weather worsening.

POLICE

When it emerged that Martha had spent most of her life in Merson Hall asylum, a now closed-down institution for the mentally ill, Ruth became even more concerned for her baby's safety.

While the search for Alfie and Martha continued, Peggy paid a visit to Gwen to ask her about the incident earlier that day. But Gwen denied knowing Martha, so Peggy had no option but to leave with her questions still unanswered. Meanwhile, Martha was out on the moors in the biting cold, singing weakly to try to comfort the crying baby and at the same time experiencing flashbacks.

The deluded woman 'saw' David, her handsome young lover of many years before, sitting beside her in his soldier's uniform. The couple talked about how they would tell her parents that she was pregnant and he reassured her that everything would be fine and soon they would be married.

● Leading the search for Ruth Goddard's baby son Alfie, when he was abducted by nursing home resident Martha Travis, was a police officer played by DAVID CRELLIN, who had always been on the other side of the law in *Emmerdale* as Andy Hopwood's no-good father, Billy.

In *Where the Heart Is* baby Alfie was taken by Martha, who had been put into an asylum after falling pregnant at the age of 16. Filming at a reservoir on the moors meant a cold night for cast and crew. PAULINE JEFFERSON, as Martha, had to wade into the reservoir with the baby before Peggy (Pam Ferris) arrived to take him from her.

'It was the middle of the night in the middle of winter, and freezing,' recalls producer Kate Anthony. 'Pauline was wearing a dress with a drysuit underneath. She walked into the water with the rain and wind machines going. We got the shot and everyone was so cold and miserable that they wanted to go home.

'But, in one of the hardest moments I've ever faced, I had to tell the crew to do it again because, as Pauline walked into the water, the drysuit had filled up with air and by the end of the shot she looked like the Michelin man!'

Nursing home resident Arthur, in the same episode, was played by TONY BROUGHTON, who acted three different roles in *Coronation Street* between 1961 and 1996, including that of Alf Roberts' councillor friend Les Curry, who died after collapsing in Alf's shop.

Tony, whose father, Arthur Leslie, played original Rovers Return landlord Jack Walker in the *Street*, was married to the late June Broughton, who played doctor's wife Mrs Lowther in the serial.

• Although it was a baby girl that originally played Alfie when Ruth Goddard gave birth in episode one, the role was subsequently taken over by THOMAS JOHNSTONE.

His mother, Philippa, worked as personal assistant to United Productions managing director Vernon Lawrence.

Just 11 weeks after his real-life birth, Thomas was making his début in front of the cameras. 'He was as good as gold and all the filming went without a hitch,' smiles Philippa. 'Sarah Lancashire seemed very relaxed with Thomas. She was very natural with him and knew how to soothe him and keep him

Ruth and Simon joined the police in the search, but night was falling and the weather worsened. The frantic young mum was driven almost to breaking point when a plastic doll, half-buried under the earth, was for a moment mistaken for baby Alfie.

Still convinced that the answer lay with Gwen Phillips, Peggy persisted with her questioning. After a great deal of soul-searching, the old woman finally confessed that Martha was her own daughter, whom her strict husband had placed in the asylum at the age of 16 after she became pregnant.

She recalled the day when Martha and David told them the news. David, she said, had been thrown out of the house by her God-fearing husband. He was killed one month later while serving in Burma during the Second World War. Martha's father had taken a belt to her, beating her black and blue before sending her away for bringing shame on the family.

Peggy told Gwen that the clue to Martha's whereabouts with Alfie must be connected with her daughter's past. The pair of them pieced the jigsaw together and, on a hunch, Peggy left for the reservoir at Diggleswade, the village in which Martha had grown up, which had been flooded after the war to form a reservoir.

Peggy reached Martha just as she was wading into the freezing water with Alfie. Dashing in after her, Peggy managed happy. She really made him laugh, too.'

There were further cast changes later. In the second series the role of Alfie was taken by JAKE MEAYS, who had already played Kim and Frank Tate's son, James, in *Emmerdale*, and in the third series young BEN HUDSON took the part of Alfie.

It was a happy reunion for mother and son as Alfie was handed back to Ruth next to the reservoir, after Peggy had found Martha wading into the freezing water with the baby.

to rescue the baby and take him safely ashore. A relieved Ruth arrived minutes later, and she and Simon were reunited with their son.

Both Martha and Alfie were cold but unhurt. After being taken back to the nursing home, Martha was visited by Jean, who now realized that Martha was her real mother, not Gwen. Martha recognized her daughter almost immediately, saying that she bore a strong resemblance to her father, David, who had been killed in the war.

A WORKING MOTHER

Peggy had always been there for her younger brother, Simon. She cared deeply for him, his wife Ruth and now their baby, Alfie. So, when he and Ruth hit rocky times, she naturally wanted to help.

After the birth of their son, Simon decided that Ruth should give up her job as a community nurse and become a full-time mother. As the pair argued bitterly about this, Simon remarked that Ruth's job was like an obsession with her. Ruth was cut to the quick and could barely speak to him.

Peggy realized that Simon was treading on dodgy ground and knew that, if he pushed hard enough, Ruth would begin to feel guilty and give up her job. She reasoned with Simon in the only way she could, by pointing out that if Ruth gave up nursing she would become a different person. 'She was born to be a nurse—she's kind and compassionate,' Peggy pleaded. Simon took his sister's words to heart and admitted to Ruth that he was wrong, saying that he only wanted her to do what made her happy.

VIC'S NEW RUGBY FIND

Vic, who acted as player-coach to local Rugby League club the Skelthwaite Scorpions, spent a day off work watching the Huddersfield rugby club train. Seeing the prowess of these players on the pitch made him realize just how far his own amateur team still had to go.

However, as he sat on the sidelines good fortune came his way in the shape of Kenny, a professional rugby player from New Zealand, who said he was desperately looking for a job. Never slow on the uptake, Vic realized how beneficial Kenny could be to the Skelthwaite team and promised him board and lodgings and a job if he would train the Scorpions in return.

A deal was struck and Vic arrived back from Huddersfield with Kenny in tow. It was not long before the colossal Kenny was creating a stir both on and off the pitch, particularly with nurse Pat Illingworth, who sat making eyes at him in the pub. Pat provided the accommodation that Kenny had been promised, while Simon gave him a job at the paper factory. Kenny became famous for leading the Scorpions in the *haka* before games, and their performance of this traditional Maori war dance often bemused the opposition.

RIGHT: *A walk along the prom was part of an enjoyable day out for Patricia (Maggie Wells), Peggy and Ruth when they went to Scarborough.*

New Zealand rugby player Kenny (Arnie Hema) was the answer to Vic Snow's prayers when he was looking to improve the Skelthwaite Scorpions team.

A DAY AT THE SEASIDE

Leaving baby Alfie with Simon, Ruth joined Peggy and Pat on a trip to a nursing conference in Scarborough. Peggy had been asked to make a speech at the conference and was the first community nurse to be asked to do so.

Although Simon was a total novice in the baby department, he coped admirably with the help of Vic and the rest of the rugby team, taking Alfie with him wherever he went—including the office and even the pub.

The three nurses arrived at the East Coast seaside resort in good spirits after making the trip in the Skelthwaite Scorpions' bright green-and-yellow minibus. While Pat and Ruth headed straight off to one of the lectures, Peggy decided to go for a run to calm her nerves.

After reaching Scarborough Castle, she pulled out her speech and rehearsed it in

• When Stephen Snow travelled to London to see Wendy Atkins again, most of the filming was actually done in Yorkshire. Two scenes featured the entrance to a hothouse, which in fact was Tropical World in Leeds. 'Stephen needed a bed for the night,' recalls production designer Alan Davies. 'We thought Tropical World was quite visual and, being a hothouse, warm for the night.'

It was in the same episode that the nurses travelled to Scarborough. Exteriors were filmed in the East Coast seaside town, but the hotel they stayed at in the series was in reality located in Harrogate, and Peggy Snow's speech to a nursing conference was shot at the former Leeds Playhouse, set within the city's university and now used as a conference centre.

front of an audience of seagulls before running across the sands. Here, Peggy spotted two men surfing, one of whom she recognized.

Meeting up later, Peggy, Ruth and Pat tucked into multi-coloured sundaes at a beachfront ice-cream parlour before taking in a tour of the town. Peggy later appeared affronted when her young sister-in-law expressed dissatisfaction with her lot in Skelthwaite. In a heart-to-heart chat, Ruth confessed that she felt she could have done more with her life if she had moved away, and that now baby Alfie had come along her fate was sealed. She was what she was—a nurse, a wife and a mother.

It was sundae best for Peggy, Patricia and Ruth as they absorbed the flavour of Scarborough during their trip to a nursing conference.

Making their way back along the promenade to the hotel, the three women bumped into the surfers that Peggy had seen earlier. The older of the two men recognized Ruth immediately and called out her name, much to Peggy's annoyance.

The surfer was Charlie, an old flame of Ruth's from her teens. They seemed delighted to see each other and arranged to meet up later that evening while Peggy and Pat attended a delegates' party. Peggy was not at all happy about this, as she

RIGHT: *Ruth expressed regret at never having broken away from Skelthwaite when she bumped into old flame Charlie (Anthony Green).*

remembered that Ruth and Charlie had once gone out with each other for two weeks when, as a 16-year-old, Ruth had broken up temporarily with Peggy's young brother, Simon.

While Peggy and Pat had a miserable evening and an early night, Ruth and Charlie had a good time talking about the old days. Ruth expressed regret at having such a conventional lifestyle and Charlie revealed that it was because of her that he had never felt able to return to Skelthwaite.

When Ruth went back to Charlie's home for a nightcap, she bombarded him with photographs of her son and her husband, leaving Charlie in no doubt of where her true allegiance lay. Exhausted by the effect of the usual night-time demands made by a young baby, Ruth fell asleep on Charlie's sofa.

Peggy, fearing the worst, gave Ruth a frosty reception when she hurried into the hotel foyer in the morning. Ruth quickly reassured her that nothing untoward had taken place,

and the nurses rushed to the conference at which Peggy was due to make her big speech, entitled 'Palliative Care in the Community—A Nurse's Eye View'.

When she took the platform, Peggy was stiff and unnatural—not at all her usual self. The audience grew restless and began to shift in their seats, whispering and laughing. Peggy, furious, gave up on her carefully constructed notes and, instead, began speaking from the heart. Soon there was not a dry eye in the hall as she told of how her mother had been allowed to die at home. When she had finished, applause rang in the air and Pat and Ruth hugged Peggy proudly. Any differences between Peggy and Ruth had entirely evaporated.

The conference over, the three women returned to Skelthwaite. During the journey Ruth reassured Peggy that she was happy with her life, her husband Simon and the choices she had made.

STEPHEN'S JOURNEY OF DISCOVERY

While Peggy was away in Scarborough, Stephen seized the opportunity to take off for London to visit Wendy Atkins. Although she was delighted to see him, events did not run as smoothly as Stephen had hoped they would. During an evening out at the local pub, Wendy's best friend, Sophie, told Stephen that his mother was responsible for the teacher resigning from her job and leaving Skelthwaite. She advised Stephen to go home and let Wendy get on with her life.

He returned north immediately, fuming at Peggy's interference. From Stephen's sullen behaviour, Peggy quickly realized that her son must have discovered what she had done. She tried to talk to him about it, but he did not want to hear. Stephen slowly began to shut Peggy out, and she confided to Vic that she thought she was losing him.

Vic eventually managed to persuade the teenager that Peggy had done what she had because she loved him—she had not intended to hurt him. Stephen decided to forgive and forget, and turned up at Peggy's birthday party with a beautiful wooden sculpture that he had made at school. All ill will was cast aside and mother and son hugged one another. They were on good terms once more.

On passing his exams, Stephen telephoned Wendy to tell her the good news and arranged to stay with her in London for a couple of days. Stephen could now maintain his contact with Wendy with Peggy's blessing. She told her son that if his relationship with Wendy was meant to work, it would—interfering mother or no interfering mother.

LOCKED OUT OF SOCIETY

Walter Charlton, who suffered from learning difficulties, lived in a flat with just a cat for company. His neighbours had always tried to support him since the death of his mother, but their patience was wearing thin and they were constantly worried as to what he would do next.

Peggy and Ruth struggled to cope with Walter's constant demands. He even turned up at Ruth's home one evening, having locked himself out when feeding birds in his garden. Ruth held a spare key to Walter's flat, so she bundled up baby Alfie and drove him home. Soon after ushering Walter into the flat, Ruth discovered his armchair ablaze —it had been left too close to a fire. Handing Alfie to Walter and telling him to take the baby outside, away from danger, Ruth went to tackle the flames.

At that moment Vic and Simon, on their way home from the pub, spotted Walter and dashed over to help. Simon was furious that Alfie had been put at risk. Back at home, he tore into Ruth angrily, telling her that she

LEFT: *Ruth was confronted with a burning armchair when she took Walter Charlton back to the flat where he had lived since the death of his mother.*

TOP: *Vic came to the rescue with a fire extinguisher to tackle the flames after spotting trouble at Walter's flat as he walked back from the pub with Simon.*

should not mix Alfie with her job, which he considered a 'bloody obsession'.

The following morning, while Ruth ignored Simon, Walter was up bright and early to go to the rubbish dump, where he found himself a replacement armchair. Pleased with his find, he made his way home, pushing the chair along in an old wire shopping trolley.

Meanwhile, unknown to Walter he was the subject of a meeting between Ruth, Peggy and his occupational therapist, Louise Winters. Peggy, who said she felt pushed to the limit by Walter's latest incident, insisted that he should be placed in sheltered accommodation, despite Ruth's protests that he would hate that.

Initially unconvinced of the need to remove Walter from the Care in the Community scheme, Louise changed her mind after being shown around his home and seeing the damage that had been caused. Ruth broke the news to Walter gently, painting a rosy picture of the proposed move. He accepted the situation readily as soon as he was told that he would be able to take his cat, visit the pub and generally 'live like a king'.

His happiness was short-lived, however. Louise could only find accommodation for him in Leeds, as everywhere in Skelthwaite was full. Walter was devastated, and even Peggy became remorseful that he would have to leave the place where he had lived all his life. She invited Walter, who had given her a birthday card, to her party that night.

Deeply upset at the prospect of having to move out of Skelthwaite, that evening Walter ran through the falling snow to the remote moorland house that had been his childhood home, where he cried out in distress to his long-departed mother.

On his return to town, whilst walking through the streets he came across Simon coming out of a shop with a crate of champagne and wine for Peggy's birthday party. Unaware that Walter had been invited, Simon handed him a bottle of wine, advising him to 'keep his head down' and not bother people in order to prove that he was capable of living on his own. Walter clutched the bottle and went off home, only to find that he had locked himself out yet again. Taking Simon's words to heart, Walter sat down on the doorstep, defeated, as the freezing cold bit into him.

Meanwhile Peggy's birthday celebrations were in full swing, with all her family and friends enjoying themselves. However, both Peggy and Ruth were becoming concerned that Walter had not turned up, so they decided to go and fetch him. By the time they arrived at his flat, Walter was unconscious and near to death from exposure, but Ruth saved his life by applying artificial respiration. An ambulance was quickly called and Walter was rushed to hospital, where he recovered from his ordeal.

PEGGY'S BEST BIRTHDAY PRESENT

Peggy had awoken on her birthday morning with a broad smile as daughter Lucy delivered her presents and cards. It would have been a perfect morning, had it not been for the animosity that Stephen was still showing towards his mother at this time, over her interference in his romance with Wendy. He did his best to wish his mother a happy birthday and Peggy did her best to respond with a happy smile.

As the day progressed, preparations got under way for the evening's festivities, with Peggy cleaning, Vic sorting out his top priority —the ale—and Ruth whipping up some delicious dips. As they worked, Peggy told Vic of her fear that she was losing Stephen. Later, she was made to feel this even more keenly when Stephen returned home from sitting a crucial exam and could hardly spare the time to mention it to her.

Vic did his best to smooth things over, impressing on Stephen how much he was upsetting his mother. 'If you're old enough to sleep with your teacher, you're old enough to stop hurting people,' he told him bluntly. Vic's message obviously hit home and made Stephen think. That night Stephen gave Peggy her best birthday present ever—his forgiveness and the beautiful wooden carving that he had made at school.

A FARMER SOWS HIS OATS

When Peggy and Ruth were called out to a lonely farmhouse, set on an island in the middle of a motorway, they had no idea that one of their most embarrassing challenges awaited them.

Ruddy-faced pig farmer Fred Fowles was unco-operative, telling the two nurses he had no idea why they had been sent for. As he led the way through the filthy house to his wife's room, Ruth and Peggy's eyes grew wider with each room they entered—food, dirty dishes and clothes were strewn around everywhere.

They found Elsa Fowles lying in bed, unwashed and smelly. When questioned about her ailment, the tearful woman

Peggy and Ruth trod carefully at a pig farm.

eventually confessed that she wanted Peggy and Ruth to do something about her husband's sexual demands.

Although this was certainly not in their job description, they agreed to talk to him. The sullen pig farmer appeared rather confused at first, but he finally got the message when Peggy suggested that he could be less 'pushy in the bedroom' and Ruth advised him to 'buy a magazine'. When they had finished, he walked out of the room without uttering a word and they breathed a joint sigh of relief.

The two nurses then left for town to buy some soap and shampoo to clean his wife up. It appeared that the situation was beginning to look up when Ruth spotted farmer Fred in the high street carrying an enormous bouquet of deep red carnations.

The location used for the episode about a pig farmer cheating on his wife appeared two years later in the docu-soap *Britain's Worst Roads*, which featured the farm that lies on land between two sides of the M62 in West Yorkshire.

In *Where the Heart Is* farmer's wife Elsa Fowles was played by MARJORIE YATES, whose television appearances over three decades include roles in Colin Welland's play *Kisses at Fifty* and the parliamentary serial *Annie's Bar*. Top judge's daughter CAROLYN PICKLES, who acted the farmer's mistress, Barbara Figgis, has played Simone in six series of the sitcom *May to December*, DCI Kim Reid in *The Bill*, Lady Ramsay in *The Tales of Para Handy* and Jane Rhodes in *Castles*.

In the same episode of *Where the Heart Is*, Hoxton Giants' rugby coach, Colin Butler, was acted by BOB MASON, who in the 'seventies joined *Coronation Street* as cornershop-owner Renée Bradshaw's younger brother Terry, who had a brief romance with Gail Platt. A decade later he had become a regular writer for the serial. More recently he played Morris in *Once Upon a Time in the North* and the local policeman, Sgt Eddie Slater, in *The Lakes*.

Assuming that the flowers were meant for his wife by way of an apology, while they bathed Elsa, Peggy and Ruth informed her of the surprise her husband was planning. They had intended the news to cheer the poor woman up, but it had quite the opposite effect. She burst into tears and revealed that her husband had been seeing someone else for the past three months.

Elsa even had receipts detailing all the expensive gifts he had lavished on her. Peggy and Ruth were amazed to see that Fred had not only taken the woman to Walt Disney World in Florida but had also bought her a new television set, a microwave and a bed.

Elsa had taken to her bed in protest, in an attempt to make her husband take notice of her. She reasoned that, if he thought there was something really wrong with her, he might show some interest. All the money the couple had been paid as compensation for the noise from the motorway traffic had been spent on a woman whose name she did not know, but whose address she had found.

For a second time, Elsa called on Peggy and Ruth to do something that was quite outside their normal responsibilities. She asked them to visit the woman and tell her to leave her husband alone. Feeling sorry for Elsa, they agreed to do this, but to their

extreme embarrassment they discovered that the lady in question was none other than Barbara Figgis, the dinner lady at Peggy's daughter Lucy's school.

Barbara was shocked to hear that her lover had a wife. He had claimed to be a wealthy widower called Harris. Barbara said her relationship with the farmer was not an affair but a simple business arrangement—he provided her with luxuries and money and she provided him with sex. She had only gone along with this to provide for her three children, after finding it hard to raise them on her own on a very low income. When Barbara promised never to see the philandering pig farmer again, Peggy assured her that the matter would go no further.

With the problem now behind her, Elsa was like a new woman. On her husband's return home, he was amazed to find a clean and tidy house and a wife who had made plans for a night of romance and passion.

LEFT: *Peggy faced one of her trickiest tasks when she found pig farmer Fred Fowles (Fred Pearson) neglecting his wife, Elsa, and showering another woman with his attentions.*

A DAY OF CELEBRATION

Stephen and Vic Snow were men living on the edge. While Stephen waited with frayed nerves for the exam results he needed for a place at university, Vic was psyching himself up for the Skelthwaite Scorpions' big match against the team's old adversaries, the Hoxton Giants.

Every morning, Stephen had been dashing for the post, but on match day he was beaten to it by Lucy, who found his results and hid them in her bedroom—she knew that if her brother had done well in his exams he would be leaving Skelthwaite, and she did not want him to go.

Unaware of Lucy's plot, Stephen had made his way down to the sports field for the big match. Vic was already there, watching Kenny practise his kicks before the opposition arrived. Vic was furious when he realized that the Hoxton Giants were fielding Graham Shuttleworth, who had professional experience with Huddersfield. He argued in vain that this was not fair.

A good home crowd cheered the Scorpions on and jeered loudly when the Giants brought Kenny down in a vicious tackle that broke his arm. Things were looking bleak for the Scorpions, until Shuttleworth was given a red card and sent off the pitch for punching a player. This came after

Scorpions player Dick Lampard, who worked at the paper factory, remembered that Shuttleworth left Huddersfield after discovering his wife in the sauna with a youth team player and taunted him about this.

The Scorpions began to close the narrow gap and eventually snatched victory after Stephen made a try and Vic scored with a magnificent kick—his last as a player.

In the best of traditions, the Scorpions and their supporters gathered in the pub to celebrate the team's win. This turned into a double celebration when Peggy arrived with Stephen's exam results, having foiling Lucy's plans to keep her brother in Skelthwaite.

All the locals cheered their team on as the Skelthwaite Scorpions locked horns on the rugby pitch with their local rivals, the Hoxton Giants.

ARNIE PITCHES IN

Introducing a Kiwi rugby player, Kenny, into the story was an idea that came to creator Ashley Pharoah while he was on the trip to New Zealand during which he finalized the first script for *Where the Heart Is*.

The casting director contacted Mick Murphy, former vice-president of Rugby League club the Huddersfield Giants, saying that he was looking for a player of New Zealand Maori origin who was living in the North of England. As a result, former professional ARNIE HEMA, who was then employed as a social worker in Halifax, was auditioned and cast in the role.

'I thought at first that I was being set up for *You've Been Framed*!' laughs Arnie. 'The producer explained that the character, Kenny, had to perform the *haka*, a traditional Maori war dance, before the game. This is thrown down as a challenge to the opposition.'

Arnie had moved to England in 1984 to play as a professional for Sheffield Eagles Rugby League club, but he later returned to New Zealand before coming back to England in 1989 to play for Mansfield, which later changed its name to Nottingham City. His last semi-professional season was in 1995.

The Halifax children's home at which Arnie worked changed its rotas specially to accommodate his filming schedules. The character Kenny made a brief return to *Where the Heart Is* during the second series.

WHO'S WHO
IN SKELTHWAITE

PEGGY SNOW
(Pam Ferris)

• Margaret 'Peggy' Goddard, born in January 1952, was just 15 when her mother died of ovarian cancer. It was then left to Peggy to bring up her little brother, Simon, 14 years her junior. With responsibility thrust upon her from an unusually early age, she later became dedicated to a career as a carer.

Peggy worked as a midwife before becoming a community nurse in her home town of Skelthwaite in 1977. Married to paper factory worker Vic Snow, she gave birth to their son Stephen two years later, by which time her father had remarried. In 1988 daughter Lucy was born.

The couple's marriage is strong and they celebrated their silver wedding anniversary in 1998. Vic was angry that Peggy had not confided in him about her anxiety that she might have the disease from which her mother had died. But her fears were dispelled when she discovered that she simply had fibroids.

It was an honour for Peggy, as a nursing sister, to become the first community nurse to be invited by the UK Central Council for

Nursing, Midwifery and Health Visiting to speak at their conference, held in Scarborough in 1997. However, she became so flustered about this that in the end she ripped up her prepared speech on 'Palliative Care in the Community— A Nurse's Eye View' and spoke personally and movingly of her mother's death.

Peggy worked with her brother Simon's wife, Ruth, but their long friendship was tested on the occasion when Vic broke his ankle by trapping it in machinery at Simon's factory. Away from her nursing duties, Peggy has found great satisfaction in taking Italian language classes and spending two weeks on a residential course in Harrogate. She is also often to be seen jogging around Skelthwaite.

RUTH GODDARD
(Sarah Lancashire)

• Staff nurse Ruth Goddard, born in 1966, was also just 15 when she lost one of her parents. Her father died, and her mother later remarried and emigrated to Australia. Ruth married childhood sweetheart Simon, and has worked for many years with his elder sister, Peggy Snow, at Skelthwaite Health Centre.

Ruth has a wicked sense of humour but could find nothing to laugh about when Simon, who owns the town's paper factory, suggested that she stop working after giving birth to their son Alfie in November 1996. Only the intervention of Peggy prevented a serious marital crisis. However, Ruth's relationship with her colleague and sister-in-law turned frosty after Peggy's husband, Vic, broke his ankle at the factory.

On a happier note, Ruth mended fences by making up with her estranged grand-mother, Nell, who had not kept in touch since the death of her son. Ruth and Simon even gave Nell a home for a while.

But the break-up of Ruth's marriage was signalled when she miscarried her second baby. Instead of coming closer in their grief, she and Simon grew apart and eventually split up. She then made the decision to go to Australia in the hope of being reunited with her mother.

VIC SNOW
(Tony Haygarth)

SIMON GODDARD
(Thomas Craig)

• Factory worker Vic Snow, born in 1952, has a rock-solid marriage to district nurse Peggy, but slightly resents working for her brother, Simon, at Goddard's Paper Products.

Much of his spare time is taken up with the Skelthwaite Scorpions rugby club, which he played for, as did his father before him. However, Vic finally stopped playing in 1997 —scoring with the final kick of a game against arch-rivals the Hoxton Giants—but subsequently continued as the team's coach. He masterminded the Scorpions' fundraising to build a clubhouse and eventually accepted that the players' dwindling interest in the team meant a merger with the Giants to form the Giant Scorpions.

Vic ended up with his leg in plaster after breaking his ankle on machinery at the factory. But he was not so quick to see that Peggy was ill, and was shocked when she told him about her cancer scare, which fortunately turned out to be nothing more than fibroids. When they were celebrating their 25th wedding anniversary in 1998, he made her promise to share everything with him in future.

It came as a surprise when Vic's first love, Angela Smith, arrived in Skelthwaite to visit her sick father. He was happy to walk her across the golf course, their old courting ground, and exchange news, but there was never any question of the flames being rekindled—he only has eyes for Peggy.

• Paper factory owner Simon Goddard, born in 1966, was brought up by his sister Peggy after their mother died of ovarian cancer when he was just a baby. He married his childhood sweetheart, Ruth, and later joined the ranks of Skelthwaite's entrepreneurs when he set up his own business, Goddard's Paper Products, which manufactures toilet rolls and kitchen paper, its major market being the United States.

Simon, who likes to be thought of as the benevolent boss, sponsors the local rugby team, but he can be brash and undiplomatic. After the birth of son Alfie in 1996, his blunt suggestion that Ruth give up her job as a community nurse to become a full-time mother was met with hostility.

He had greater problems to contend with when business at the factory slackened off but was saved by an order from Denmark. Later, he put expansion plans into operation, hiring outsider Alison Storey as a strategy consultant and taking on local teenager Henry Green as trainee manager. But he overstretched himself and ended up remortgaging his house—without telling Ruth.

Simon's domestic life was already in turmoil. When Ruth fell pregnant with their second child but then suffered a miscarriage, he was unable to offer her the support she needed. The couple ended up separating and Simon moved into the factory, unable to accept that his marriage was over. It was a shock when Ruth left Skelthwaite for Australia to see her mother for the first time in almost 20 years.

STEPHEN SNOW (William Ash *(top picture)* **and Jason Done)**

• Born in January 1979, Skelthwaite High School pupil Stephen Snow planned to leave his home town of Skelthwaite and study at university. During his second year of A-levels, he fell for teacher Wendy Atkins, just three years his senior. But his mother, Peggy, threatened to report Wendy's affair if she did not leave town quietly.

Classmate Deborah Alliss continued to set her cap at Stephen, but he never regarded her as a real girlfriend. He started an English and drama degree course at Bristol University but decided he wanted to switch to psychology and was advised to take a year out to gain some relevant experience.

Returning home, Stephen found voluntary work in nearby Haleford at the Lord Harris School, for children with emotional and behavioural difficulties, and fell for Skelthwaite's new district nurse, Jacqui Richards.

After the couple split up, Stephen had a fling with businesswoman Alison Storey, but they got back together when Jacqui announced she was pregnant. Stephen abandoned his university plans, took a job sweeping up at his Uncle Simon's paper factory and moved into a rented house with Jacqui. He was overjoyed at the birth of their son Jake.

JACQUI RICHARDS
(Marsha Thomason)

LUCY SNOW
(Jessica Baglow)

• Feisty, newly qualified registered nurse Jacqui Richards arrived at Skelthwaite Health Centre in 1997 after graduating from Leeds University and spending a year on a hospital's geriatric ward. Apart from a short placement at a community health practice during her training, she had no experience of working in the community—or in a rural area.

In Skelthwaite, Jacqui tried to put a textbook approach into practice and was quick to mock the other nurses' apparent wariness of computers as well as their preference for the traditional uniform. However, she soon learned the importance of treating patients as human beings and not simply as names on a list.

Jacqui found lodgings with fellow nurse Patricia Illingworth and fell for her colleague Peggy's son, Stephen Snow. But she and Stephen eventually split up when she went on a course in Leeds and he was due to start at Bristol University. On her return, Jacqui announced that she was pregnant and said she would bring the baby up by herself. But Stephen persuaded her that he loved her and wanted to be with her, so the couple rented a house together and Jacqui gave birth to their son Jake in 1999.

• Schoolgirl Lucy Snow, born in 1988, loves it when she gets the chance to go out with her mother, district nursing sister Peggy, on her rounds. Lucy has always been very close to her big brother, Stephen. She even intercepted his A-level results in an attempt to prevent him from leaving Skelthwaite to go off to university.

In 1998 Lucy moved up from the town's junior school to the high school, where Stephen later started work as a classroom assistant.

WENDY ATKINS
(Susannah Wise)

- Skelthwaite High School excelled in drama when newly qualified teacher Wendy Atkins taught English there. But her affair with sixth-former Stephen Snow brought her employment at the school to an untimely end.

When Stephen's mother, Peggy, found out about the relationship, she issued Wendy with an ultimatum that resulted in her dumping Stephen and returning to London, having told her headteacher that her mother was ill.

When Stephen discovered the truth, he followed her. Wendy was pleased to see him, but a friend of hers told Stephen that it was his mother who had forced Wendy to leave Skelthwaite. Stephen returned home, but later paid Wendy a celebratory visit after receiving his A-level results.

PATRICIA ILLINGWORTH
(Maggie Wells)

- Part-time nurse Patricia Illingworth takes pride in her job at Skelthwaite Health Centre and is a calming influence in times of crisis. Her only vice appears to be over-eating.

Many years after the premature death of her husband Alan, whose picture remains on her mantelpiece, Pat fell for Kiwi rugby player Kenny, who became her lodger. However, Kenny soon returned to his native New Zealand.

She found another lodger in newly qualified district nurse Jacqui Richards, but was pleased when Kenny made a brief return visit to Skelthwaite. She eventually found a new love in Gerry Flint, another rugby player.

KENNY
(Arnie Hema)

• A Maori from Paekakariki in New Zealand, Kenny had travelled around Europe and was hoping to work as a rugby player in Britain but was unable to get a trial. Skelthwaite Scorpions' player-coach, Vic Snow, met Kenny and found him accommodation with Pat Illingworth as well as a job at brother-in-law Simon Goddard's paper factory, in return for Kenny both playing for the team and training the players.

Kenny's trademark was leading the Scorpions in the *haka*, the Maori war dance customarily performed in his home country to inspire the team and frighten the opposition. Pat developed a soft spot for Kenny, but in due course he returned to New Zealand. She was pleased when he came back to Skelthwaite briefly for the opening of the Scorpions' club-house—and exchanged a passionate kiss with her.

DEBORAH ALLISS
(Laura Crossley)

• Sixth-former Deborah Alliss thought she was going out with Stephen Snow, but he was really using her as a smokescreen for his relationship with teacher Wendy Atkins. Debs played Stella—badly—alongside Stephen in their school production of *A Streetcar Named Desire*.

Later, she was pleased when he returned from university after giving up his course, but all too soon she found that he was dating young community nurse Jacqui Richards. Debs earned money by babysitting Alfie Goddard during the day and working as a barmaid at the Skelthwaite Arms in the evenings.

Finally accepting that she was never going to get together with Stephen, Debs fell for the charms of another former schoolfriend, Henry Green. But she tried a little too hard to push him into getting engaged and moving into a flat with her.

HENRY GREEN
(Andrew Knott)

NELL
(Hazel Douglas)

- Always in awe of schoolfriend Stephen Snow, Henry Green longed to enjoy the same success with the girls and was infatuated with Deborah Alliss. She, however, only had eyes for Stephen.

On leaving school, Henry worked in the local supermarket—where he had previously had a part-time job. He proved his dedication to Debs when he joined the Skelthwaite menfolk on a fishing trip to Whitby and turned down the sexual favours offered by a teenager he met there, called Susan.

Debs subsequently saw Henry's caring side when he saved an old woman's embarrassment at the supermarket by untucking her skirt from her knickers without making a fuss. The young couple started going out together, but in the end Henry, who by then was working as trainee manager at the paper factory, had to pluck up the courage to tell Debs he was not ready to get engaged and move in with her, after she began to push the relationship along too quickly for him.

- Ruth Goddard's grandmother, Nell, had had nothing to do with Ruth since the death of her son, Ruth's father, after which Ruth's mother had remarried and moved to Australia. Neither did Nell approve of Ruth's choice of husband.

Feeling that the rift should be healed after so many years, Ruth visited Nell in Harrogate and told her that she should see her great-grandson, Alfie. Fiercely independent Nell was not quick to make peace and resented the suggestion that she was having difficulty in living by herself.

However, after bruising a hip she agreed to stay with Ruth and Simon. Eventually Nell sold her house in Harrogate and moved into sheltered accommodation at Pine Tree House in Skelthwaite, before dying in 1999.

DICK LAMPARD
(William Travis)
CHERYL LAMPARD
(Kathryn Hunt)

• Bachelor Dick Lampard, who played rugby for the Skelthwaite Scorpions, was employed at Simon Goddard's paper factory. But he was sacked from his job after sending kitchen paper instead of toilet rolls to a client in America —a mistake that resulted in the customer's toilets becoming blocked—and then going to pub landlord George Cooper's funeral when he was supposed to be at work sorting the problem out. Dick was subsequently reinstated, however, when Simon accepted that he had overreacted.

Dick found the love of his life when he joined the lads for a fishing trip to Whitby and serenaded skipper's assistant Cheryl with 'Love Me Tender' at a karaoke evening. Having spent the night with him in his hotel room, Cheryl went off to work. She then rushed to wave goodbye to the lads as they left the hotel in their minibus, but got there just too late. Shortly afterwards, however, she tracked Dick down in Skelthwaite—and stayed.

This upturn in Dick's life coincided with the horror of his running over a young boy while driving a factory delivery van. Gary Kettle, who had run out in front of the vehicle, later died in hospital and Dick was charged with reckless driving. Fortunately, he escaped jail when it was discovered that the new crossing was not adequately signposted. Cheryl and Dick married in 1998, but their attempts at starting a family were hindered by Dick's low sperm count.

• As assistant to the skipper at a Whitby boat-hire company, Cheryl met Dick Lampard when he and the Skelthwaite men arranged a fishing trip to the East Coast seaside town. They shared a passionate night together, but Dick left for home the following day and Cheryl was too late to wave him off.

After writing to Dick and failing to get any answer to her telephone calls, she headed for Skelthwaite and found her seaside Romeo a changed man—he was coming to terms with running over a boy, who had subsequently died. She helped him to get through this bad time but at one point considered returning to Whitby. Dick assured her that he would change and she agreed to marry him.

The couple married in a register office, although Cheryl had shocked Dick shortly beforehand by confessing that she had been married to a man called Gavin at the age of 18. The newlyweds settled in Dick's flat and Cheryl found a job at an estate agent's.

SANDRA HARRISON
(Melanie Kilburn)
KEITH HARRISON
(Neil McCaul)

• Sandra, the younger sister of Vic Snow, had been at school with her brother's wife-to-be, Peggy, and the two women had subsequently trained as nurses together. But when Sandra married Bradford man Keith Harrison she went to live in that city, where she gave birth to their son Craig and daughter Donna.

In 1998, having concentrated for years on bringing up her children, Sandra decided that she wanted to make something of her life. Returning to Skelthwaite with Craig, she arrived on Vic's doorstep but was soon to find husband Keith hot on her heels.

The Harrisons decided to settle in Skelthwaite and lived temporarily in a caravan outside the Snows' house, before converting a derelict barn. With a view to picking up her career again, Sandra retrained as a nurse.

• Still besotted with wife Sandra, Keith Harrison followed her to Skelthwaite when she became dissatisfied with her lot and returned to her home town after 18 years of living with him and their children in Bradford, where he owned a DIY business.

Realizing that she was serious about staying in Skelthwaite, he earmarked a derelict barn for conversion and set about planning the family's future there. He also went into the architectural salvage business as a means of earning money.

Impetuous and inclined to sulk, Keith is used to ducking and diving, but he has an optimistic outlook on life. As far as he is concerned, Sandra is just as attractive and sexy as she was on the day they married.

CRAIG HARRISON
(Alex Carter)

• Born and brought up in Bradford, schoolboy Craig Harrison was unhappy at being dragged to Skelthwaite by his mother, Sandra. When his father came to find them he thought this meant the family would return home, but was shocked when his parents decided to settle in Skelthwaite, where his mother used to live.

This insecurity led Craig to play truant, and a teacher's suspicion that he might be dyslexic resulted in his being referred to a child psychologist. In the end he accepted that his parents were happy and began to settle down in his new environment.

TERRY
(Simon Ashley)

• Beer-swilling plasterer and rugby player Terry has a habit of saying the wrong thing. He follows a bad defeat with the words: 'There's always next week.' Even when Skelthwaite Arms landlord George Cooper died, Terry's main concern was who would be running the pub.

Although his sexuality has never been called into question, while all the other men were gazing at the slim, trim young women walking through the foyer of the Whitby hotel where they were staying during a fishing trip, daydreaming Terry was staring up at the plasterwork on the ceiling.

He failed to provide emotional support when Dick Lampard killed a boy in a road accident, and finally had to accept that he could no longer continue hanging around Dick's flat drinking and watching television when his bachelor friend married Cheryl.

ALISON STOREY
(Katrina Levon)

• When strategy consultant Alison Storey was brought in by Goddard's Paper Products to help sort out the company's finances, she soon launched into a fling with Simon Goddard's young nephew, Stephen Snow. This earned her the cold shoulder from Jacqui Richards, who had split up with Stephen but, on her return from a course, later became reunited with him.

Simon's wife Ruth suspected that Alison was having an affair with her husband, but in fact Alison did not try to make a conquest of Simon until he and Ruth had gone their separate ways. Soon coming to his senses, Simon gave Alison the brush-off, whereupon she decided it was time to move on.

WALTER CHARLTON
(Graham Turner)

• A combination of learning difficulties and continence problems caused Walter Charlton to become reliant on the community around him following the death of his mother. Peggy and Ruth soon discovered that he was incapable of looking after himself, when he locked himself out of his flat and accidentally set his armchair alight. Walter almost died after again locking himself out in the freezing cold. It was only the arrival of Ruth, who administered the kiss of life, that saved him.

Peggy insisted that Walter be found sheltered accommodation, but because there was nowhere locally, he had to go to Leeds. Later, he was glad to return to Skelthwaite when a place was found for him in the group home. Simon once employed Walter to sweep up at the paper factory—paying him in beer so that he could sidestep losing his benefits.

1997–8

After winning the hearts of viewers with its first series, *Where the Heart Is* and its characters returned in April 1998 for an extended run of ten episodes. This time, Ashley Pharoah devised the main storylines for the entire series, together with Vicky Featherstone and script editor Diederick Santer, but wrote only four of the scripts.

'I thought I was in danger of burning myself out otherwise,' he explains. 'The first series had been very much my voice, so I was also intrigued about how the programme would hold up with other writers coming on board. We learned that other people could take those characters and that world, and bring their own voices and their own concerns to the writing. We also found that the individual stories in each episode worked best when they echoed the serial stories in the same episode. It took a lot of care to make that happen.'

The new series, on which Ashley was joined by scriptwriters Tony Jordan, Peter Bowker, Stephen Greenhorn and Michael Wynne, went a step further in exploring the characters of Peggy and Ruth. Unfolding stories included Peggy's fear that she might have ovarian cancer, from which her mother had died when she was a teenager, and the reconciliation between Ruth and her paternal grandmother, who had not seen one another since the district nurse's widowed mother had remarried and emigrated to Australia.

'It was interesting for me,' says Pam Ferris, 'that Peggy, remembering her own mother's death, thought that she might have the same illness. I read up a bit about ovarian cancer. It's known as the "silent killer", because you don't start getting the symptoms until it's too late. It creeps up on you and suddenly you have no time left. I spoke to Margaret Tiffany—who's been a constant help and support on all medical issues—and she gave me some books to help me bone up on the subject. I didn't speak to anyone who had experienced the illness personally, because I think that would have clouded Peggy's spontaneous reaction. I had a good handle on Peggy and knew most of the medical facts, and I think those two elements were enough.'

The series began with a rift between the two central families after Vic broke his ankle when his foot got caught in machinery at Simon's paper factory. It also introduced young community nurse Jacqui Richards, who had to get used to rural life and traditional ways of working after training in Leeds. Stephen, deciding to give up the idea of going to university, returned home and fell for her. Also, minor characters from the first series were given bigger stories, such as Deborah finally accepting that Stephen was not interested in her, and falling instead for Henry.

'We wanted to keep up the banter between Peggy and Ruth, which was something viewers particularly enjoyed in the first series, according to research,' says Ashley. 'But ten hours of people being good friends doesn't make great drama. In fact, Pam Ferris and Sarah Lancashire came to me and asked if we could get some conflict into their friendship. So that was their idea—and they were absolutely right.'

Just as the nurses had travelled to Scarborough in the previous series, this time the men of Skelthwaite went on a fishing trip outing to Whitby. While they were there, Dick met Cheryl, who later followed him back home and became a regular character in the series. But there was also guilt—and the prospect of imprisonment —for Dick after he killed a boy in a road accident while driving a paper factory van. Another trip saw Peggy and Vic celebrating their silver wedding anniversary in the Lake District.

'Although we didn't see very much of Dick and Terry in the first series, we always viewed them as vital components of the set-up,' explains producer Kate Anthony. 'We decided to expand their roles in the second series and learn more about them, especially Dick. That was a natural progression. We also made a conscious decision to find out more about Simon because he was such a complex character. We wanted to give greater insight into why he set up the factory and how his marriage worked so well. He isn't just a brusque boss—he's also Peggy's brother and Ruth's husband.'

The timespan of the stories again reflected when the episodes were filmed, from the autumn of 1997 to the spring of the following year. Spending such a long time filming in West Yorkshire led Pam Ferris and her husband, actor Roger Frost, to move from Essex to London, which made it easier to travel by train to and from home when there was time off—usually about three days every two weeks. 'We had been thinking about moving back to London,' says Pam, 'and the fact that they commissioned a second series allowed us financially to do that, so I was very grateful. I thank all 12 million viewers for my new house!'

LEFT: *Peggy and Vic celebrated their silver wedding anniversary during the second series—giving Pam Ferris and Tony Haygarth a trip to the Lake District.*

A SHY HEART-THROB

WILLIAM ASH quickly became a heart-throb when he appeared as teenager Stephen Snow in *Where the Heart Is*. On screen, he discarded girlfriend Deborah Alliss for teacher Wendy Atkins, then fell for community nurse Jacqui Richards. Off screen, he won an army of female admirers.

But any bashfulness about this adoration was nothing compared with what William had been through shortly beforehand when he made *Bare Necessities*, a television forerunner to *The Full Monty* in which he played one of five Sheffield miners-turned-strippers. 'I was terrified,' recalls William, 'but the other actors helped me get over my shyness.'

Acting was never William's ambition, until his dreams of becoming a professional footballer, for his home-town team of Oldham, were shattered by a broken leg at the age of 16.

Encouraged by a teacher to concentrate on drama, William built upon the acting experience he had been gaining at Oldham Theatre Workshop since 1986. This had led to roles in *Children's Ward* and the factory drama *Making Out*, in which he acted Nicky and his mother was played by Melanie Kilburn, who joined *Where the Heart Is* as Stephen Snow's aunt for the third series.

William's first 'grown-up' role was as young squaddie Jack Stubbs in two series of *Soldier, Soldier*. At about the same time, he was in director Ken Loach's acclaimed film *Raining Stones*.

He acted alongside Billie Whitelaw in the television series *Born to Run* before landing the role of Stephen Snow, a character he saw as 'dead warm, honest and hard-working'. After two series of *Where the Heart Is*, William decided to leave in order to further his career.

CLOSING TIME FOR GEORGE

When Skelthwaite Arms landlord George Cooper died, the regulars put thoughts of what would happen to the pub to the back of their minds and went along to say their final goodbyes at his funeral.

George had been a patient of Peggy and Ruth's and both he and his wife of 40 years, Mary, had been well respected members of the community. But at the funeral Peggy was concerned to see Mary showing very little emotion. While her daughter, Anne, wept openly during the church service, Mary sat stony-faced throughout.

Later, back at the pub, much to Anne's embarrassment her mother began to act in an entirely inappropriate manner, drinking heavily and dancing wildly before falling to the floor and sobbing loudly. Anne and Ruth then walked Mary home. After being left alone as she had asked, Mary gathered up George's clothes and took them into the garden to burn. To the great concern of her neighbours, she sat impassively in front of the flaming bonfire.

Peggy was called round to help Mary. She sat and listened as Mary explained how she had discovered a pile of love-letters in among George's old clothes. These revealed that over the years her husband had been conducting a long-distance love affair with a woman he had first met on a brewery course in Germany in 1965.

Mary was devastated. Even though she had been with George for so long, she now realized that she never really knew him. She felt cheated by his death, because it meant nothing could ever be resolved. She would continue to live a lie for the sake of daughter Anne, who thought the world of her father. There was no reason for Anne's memory of George to be sullied, as Mary's had been.

SIMON'S U-BEND MANAGEMENT

One person who was missing from George Cooper's funeral was Vic Snow. The cause of his absence was a blunder that had been made at the paper factory by Dick Lampard and the resulting overreaction on the part of boss Simon, who was beginning to buckle under the strain of keeping his company afloat.

When a complaint was received from a valued customer in Florida, Simon discovered that Dick had sent kitchen paper instead of toilet tissue to these important American clients, causing their toilets to block. In order to pacify them, Simon promised to send out another batch at his own expense.

Furious and panic-stricken, he insisted that the replacement toilet paper order be processed immediately, banning the men from going off to attend George's funeral. Dick defiantly walked out, ignoring Simon's warning that he would be fired if he did so. Seeing how worried Simon was, Vic stayed behind to help him get the extra work done.

When Vic failed to arrive at the church, Peggy headed for the factory to confront Simon, who had been hard at work with Vic attempting to repair a broken machine. Vic was still with the machine when Simon went off to his office to fetch

After performing an impromptu rendition of 'My Way' at the factory, Vic slipped, trapping his foot in a machine roller, and ended up with a broken ankle.

a toolbox. While he was searching for it, Peggy stormed in, furious because Vic had been made to miss the funeral.

As the pair argued, Vic, becoming bored with waiting around, began walking across the top of the machine, singing a mean rendition of Frank Sinatra's 'My Way'. But he slipped, causing the mechanical roller to lurch into action and trap his foot.

When the bickering Peggy and Simon finally heard Vic's agonized cries for help, they ran to his aid and an ambulance was called. At hospital, he was found to have a broken ankle that would require surgery and, much to Vic's dismay, a short stay in hospital. On going home, he would be confined to a wheelchair before progressing to crutches.

While Vic was forced to take it easy, tempers were running high between Simon and the rest of the factory's workforce, who were angry about both the accident and Dick's dismissal. The incident also set Peggy and Ruth at loggerheads over who was responsible. Ruth felt hurt and alone, while Simon found himself being given the cold shoulder by the Skelthwaite community.

In an effort to make amends and win back a place in his sister's good books, Simon loaned Peggy's son, Stephen—who had just returned from university—his flashy red four-wheel-drive vehicle to collect Vic from the hospital. But Peggy was furious and accused Simon of lending her son a 'death trap'.

However, her heart finally melted when she was called out to help Ruth deliver Jess and Tim Purnell's baby son. The new life brought a sense of proportion to their differences, making them seem needless and shallow. They hugged one another, happy to still be the friends they had always been.

STEERING TOWARDS DISASTER (1)

Tim Purnell was a keen motorcyclist who had broken his leg in a road accident. His heavily pregnant wife, Jess, was fed up with his hobby. She was adamant that Tim should face up to his new responsibilities and use the compensation money she believed he would be awarded after the accident to buy them a comfortable family home. But Tim had different ideas and planned to use the money to start his own motorbike business. Both their plans looked unlikely to

- Heavily pregnant Jess Purnell, wife of motorbike-mad Tim, was acted by KEELEY FORSYTH, who had previously played Nicky in two series of *The Biz* and a nurse in *Peak Practice*, as well as acting in *Children's Ward*. Keeley has since appeared in *Hollyoaks*.

come to fruition when Tim was charged with dangerous driving and issued with a summons to appear in court.

Keeping this from his wife, Tim allowed Jess to dream on. She talked about her frustration at Tim's persistence with his business plans to Ruth, when she visited to treat Tim's injuries from the accident. Jess eventually snapped on discovering the court summons hidden under their mattress. Completely hysterical, she took it out on Tim's motorbike, bashing it hard with a hammer and tipping it over.

Tim stormed off to the Skelthwaite Arms and told Stephen Snow about his problems. Meanwhile, back at home, Jess went into labour. Fortunately, Ruth had called round on a routine visit and quickly phoned for an ambulance.

However, a road block in the centre of Skelthwaite meant that the ambulance was unable to get there in time, so Ruth—who had never performed a delivery—called Peggy and the town's new GP, Dr Daniel Leeming, for help. While the young doctor was still rushing around trying to find the right address, Peggy arrived on the scene. Although it was 20 years since she had delivered a baby, she managed successfully to bring Jess's tiny son into the world.

Moments later, the doctor and Tim—pushed by Stephen in a pub barrel trolley—arrived. Hugging his wife and son, Tim realized that the time had finally come for him to grow up and set about buying a house.

STEERING TOWARDS DISASTER (2)

Traffic chaos in Skelthwaite was caused by Mary Cooper, for whom Peggy had continued to care as she adapted to life without husband George. On a routine visit Peggy was surprised to find Mary sitting in George's car inside the garage playing Everly Brothers tapes. Mary explained that, while daughter Anne was away visiting relatives, she preferred to stay 'near' George.

She also said that she had decided to take up driving again, after 30 years, and asked Peggy to accompany her on her maiden trip. Concealing her disquiet, Peggy agreed and sat in the passenger seat as Mary 'kangaroo-jumped' and stalled the car, before narrowly missing an oncoming vehicle.

It was obvious to Peggy that, after such a long absence from driving, Mary would need some expert driving tuition.

- The chaos caused by pub landlord's widow Mary Cooper in her Ford Granada led to police closing off Market Street, in the centre of Milnsbridge, which doubled as Skelthwaite High Street.

In the story, Mary swerved to avoid a rollerblading youngster and caused a lorry to jackknife, leaving the road completely blocked. The scene took a whole day to film, with stunt performers standing in as Mary and the lorry driver.

'We don't make a habit of blocking off whole roads,' says production co-ordinator Vicky Locke. 'We generally work around what's going on. But we do have to seal off the roads and involve the police if any danger to other people could be involved.'

In pointing this out she upset Mary by telling her that there was only so much she could do—she couldn't replace George.

So Mary decided to do things her own way and took to the road alone, nearly hitting both a motorcyclist and a pedestrian, before causing a lorry to jack-knife, shedding its load all over Skelthwaite High Street. Dazed and confused, Mary climbed out of the car and stumbled home. Later, with the support of Peggy and Ruth, she went to the police station and faced charges.

THE ROVER RETURNS

When Stephen reappeared on Peggy's doorstep, she was both happy and suspicious. He had been the first person in her family ever to get to university and she wondered what had gone wrong.

She was slightly reassured when Stephen told her he had not left altogether but wanted to switch from an English to a psychology degree and had been advised by his tutors to take a year out to gain some relevant experience. Stephen told his mother that home was where he belonged and asked if she could find him a voluntary placement. Peggy was delighted that her son would be staying in Skelthwaite for a while.

But Peggy subsequently felt a little hurt when Deborah let the cat out of the bag by revealing that he had made plans to work at the Lord Harris School in Haleford, which catered for children with educational and behavioural problems.

With Debs and baby Alfie Goddard in tow, Stephen arrived at the school with no appointment or interview, just bags of confidence and attitude. This approach seemed to have paid off when the headteacher agreed to give him a day's trial. Stephen was sure that he would be a success. He had youth, understanding, commitment and energy—how could he possibly fail?

However, on his first day things proved to be rather different from his expectations. Stephen threw himself into the work with great gusto, helping a group of children to paint a mural on the wall. Thinking he was doing the right thing, he singled out one boy, Clint, for praise. The boy's talent was phenomenal and Stephen complimented him on his painting of a motorbike and rider. Clint said nothing but walked off in silence.

Later that day, Stephen was dismayed to discover that the boy had totally obliterated his piece of art by throwing paint all over it. Working with emotionally and behavourially disturbed children was not turning out to be as straightforward as Stephen had expected. He didn't do too badly, though, and was overjoyed when he was allowed to continue helping at the school.

Mary Cooper (June Watson) missed her late husband, George, and only narrowly escaped being involved in an accident in her car.

ABOVE: *Andy Moore took over at the Skelthwaite Arms after the death of landlord George Cooper.*

BELOW: *Simon ignored the pub boycott, when Andy refused to allow the rugby team to change there.*

NEW LANDLORD CALLS TIME

There was trouble at the Skelthwaite Arms when new landlord Andy Moore made it clear that George's tradition of allowing the rugby club to use the pub's basement as a dressing room could not continue, claiming the brewery had other plans for the space.

This bombshell left the Scorpions indignant and desperate, not least when they had to forfeit a match after the opposition quoted Rule 9, Paragraph 4, which stated that the visiting team could count themselves the winners if the home team failed to provide adequate changing facilities.

When Vic failed to persuade Andy to change his mind, he ordered his friends to down their pints and boycott the pub until it changed its policy. The team also removed all Scorpions pictures and memorabilia from the pub.

Carried along in their mood of defiance, the men decided to follow Stephen's suggestion and apply for Lottery funding to buy their own clubhouse. One of Andy's few remaining customers was Simon, who, like himself, was an outcast.

As time went on, resentments began to dissolve and any raw edges started to heal. The lads were on a high after a fishing expedition to Whitby and, once back in Skelthwaite, were delighted to discover that Andy had had a change of heart—they could use the pub facilities after all.

SIMON HOLDS OUT AN OLIVE BRANCH

Simon soon realized that he had been rash in firing Dick Lampard, who had been not only an employee but also a mate. He tracked Dick down to the canal where he was fishing and asked him to come back to work, telling him that the factory was not the same without him. Simon then held out a further olive branch by apologizing, but Dick maintained an air of indifference.

Later, at a factory meeting, Simon once again had to eat humble pie, telling his men that he had acted the way he had only because he was so worried about the future of the business. He pleaded for their support and was heartened when Dick walked in and led the other workers in promising Simon their full backing.

JACQUI RUFFLES FEATHERS...

When Jacqui Richards arrived in Skelthwaite on a short contract as a community staff nurse, she soon created some large ripples in a small pond. With her stunning looks and self-assured manner, this 22-year-old black woman from Leeds created quite a stir among the young blood of the town, as well as ruffling Ruth's feathers on her first day at the Health Centre.

Ruth, acting as Jacqui's mentor, did her best to make the young nurse feel welcome. But after giving her a guided tour of the office and explaining the patient booking system, Ruth was fuming when Jacqui laughed at the old stagers' archaic ways and was incredulous that they didn't make use of the computers that had been installed. The newcomer also poured scorn on Ruth's parochial outlook, which she implied was the result of Ruth never moving away from her home town.

Jacqui had read all the books and leaflets on community nursing but clearly lacked practical experience. She was most put out when a patient asked her to make a pot of tea. 'I didn't go to university to be a scivvy,' Jacqui later complained to Ruth. Upset by Jacqui's

attitude, Ruth remarked to Peggy that the young nurse was obsessed with rules and computers and lacked sensitivity, but Peggy told her to trust her judgement in employing her.

Academic training did not provide newly qualified Jacqui Richards (Marsha Thomason) with the practical skills needed to work as a community nurse—as Ruth discovered.

...AND LEARNS A LESSON

Jacqui was eventually brought down a peg or two after her negligence could have resulted in a patient dying. School-teacher Adam Ponting and his wife Sarah were distraught when her cervical cancer robbed them of the chance to have a child of their own. Diagnosed with the condition while pregnant with their longed-for first child, Sarah had to have the pregnancy terminated and undergo a hysterectomy.

Sarah was locked into her own private world of grief and could not bear to let Adam in. His attempts to help, such as suggesting adoption, only made matters worse. 'I want kids out of my body—not someone else's,' she screamed at him.

When Ruth and Jacqui called on the couple, their distress was plain to see. While Jacqui re-dressed Sarah's operation scar, Ruth talked to Adam. He told her of his frustration at being shut out by his wife and how he felt that he was losing her. Before, he said, she had been like a fire, 'warm and bright and crackling… but the fire's out now'. Meanwhile, Sarah engaged Jacqui in a conversation about whether she wanted children, instead of answering Jacqui's questions on any aches and pains that she might have been experiencing.

Later that evening Ruth received an urgent call from Adam. She rushed round to the house with Jacqui to examine Sarah, who had an extremely painful leg and was becoming very breathless. Ruth suspected a deep-vein thrombosis and called for an ambulance to take Sarah to hospital. Thankfully, she arrived in time and was treated for a pulmonary embolism, caused by the thrombosis travelling to her lungs.

Jacqui was concerned that she had missed the early-warning signs of a potentially life-threatening condition on her earlier visit, while Ruth was aware that she should not have left a new nurse alone to handle a patient. Both were overjoyed to hear of Sarah's recovery. Jacqui had learned the hard way the most important rule of the job: listening.

Ruth realized that she had been hard on Jacqui and gave her some valuable advice on community nursing. 'Listen, use your intuition and instincts—you only have one shot, so you have to get it right.'

- STEVE HUISON, who played suicidal Lomper in the hit film *The Full Monty*, played schoolteacher Adam Ponting, coping with his wife's depression after a hysterectomy, necessitated by cervical cancer, meant they could never have a child of their own.

When Henry had to walk into a lamppost in the same episode, actor ANDREW KNOTT took his cue from Rowan Atkinson. He watched the comedy star do the same thing in a *Mr Bean* video, then practised making contact with the lamppost.

'To make it look realistic, you have to walk straight into the thing without flinching,' comments Andrew. 'After all, dozy Henry doesn't know what's coming up, so you can't show that you do, either. It really hurts. You end up with bruises everywhere.'

NEW LOVE IN SKELTHWAITE…

Jacqui first met Stephen in a most unromantic way. Peggy brought the new nurse home to lance the large boil that had appeared on her teenage son's bottom, as he had forbidden either his mother or 'Auntie' Ruth to perform the deed. So, with a wry smile, Peggy introduced Stephen to Jacqui. There was a distinct chemistry between the two from the start.

When Stephen spotted Jacqui at a bus stop later that evening, at the end of her first day in Skelthwaite, he offered her a lift in Simon's jeep, which he was still using. He drove Jacqui back to Leeds while Debs—by now working behind the bar at the Skelthwaite Arms in the evenings and looking after baby Alfie by day—waited in vain for him to turn up at the pub.

On the journey to Leeds, Jacqui told Stephen to lose the goatee beard he was sporting so proudly. He did, much to the relief of his father, who had been teasing him about it ever since he had returned home.

RIGHT: *Crazy golf proved to be a more appropriate pastime for Vic and Simon on their trip to Whitby, after they had given up sea fishing on choppy water.*

...AND ACROSS IN WHITBY

Overruling Simon's preference for a spot of golf, the Skelthwaite lads decided to head for Whitby to partake in a little sea fishing. Led by Vic, with his foot still in plaster, the merry band of Simon, Stephen, Dick, Terry and Henry hit the road in the Scorpions' minibus

Arriving at the seaside, the lads boarded their vessel, laughing loudly at Simon. 'It's a banana with zips,' they cried, when he turned up in the latest, most expensive-looking bright yellow sailing gear.

Not far out to sea, and with not a catch in sight, the decision was made to turn back. Simon, who had been vomiting violently over the side ever since they set off, breathed a sigh of relief, while Dick was looking forward to catching up with skipper's assistant Cheryl, the bouncy brunette who had given him the eye when they hired the boat.

After returning to their hotel for a wash and brush-up, the group made their way to the local hostelry, where Dick proceeded to serenade Cheryl with his rendition of 'Love Me Tender' in the pub's karaoke. Cheryl virtually fell into his arms, before the boat's miserable old skipper made his claim to Cheryl by punching Dick. Simon recovered some street cred with the group by coming to Dick's aid and hitting the ancient sailor in the crotch with Vic's crutch, leaving Dick and Cheryl free to share a night of passion.

Stephen and Henry left the old ones to it and escaped to find the bright lights of Whitby. As they walked along the narrow pavements, Henry confided in Stephen that he was in love with Deborah, even though she appeared to have eyes only

- SEAMUS O'NEILL, who played the skipper of the fishing boat hired by the Skelthwaite men in Whitby, had previously acted Barry Mitchell in *Albion Market*, Rob Trevor in *Brookside*, Jimmy in *EastEnders*, DC Caplan in the original *Prime Suspect* mini-series, Frank Johnson in *Families* and Tracy Preston's father-in-law, Maurice, in *Coronation Street*. He also took the role of a repugnant punter who bound and gagged Samantha Morton to a hotel-room bed in writer Kay Mellor's prostitutes drama *Band of Gold*, and has since played Emily Wylie's tyrannical father, John, in *Emmerdale*.

for him. Their search ended at the Smugglers nightspot, where Henry grew even more aggrieved at his best mate's apparent magnetism with women. While Stephen became an instant hit on the dance floor, Henry stayed out on the sidelines.

At the end of the evening, Stephen looked to be 'on a promise' with a drunken Glaswegian girl, Julie, while Henry was given the opportunity to lose his virginity with her sober blonde friend, Susan.

But things did not go according to plan. Stephen spent the night sleeping alone—his 'friend for the night' threw up in the bathroom before collapsing on the bedroom floor. Meanwhile Henry, not interested in getting intimate with anyone but Debs, was happy to spend the night just talking to Susan, who had the same problem with her friend as Henry had with Stephen. 'Everything's their own private Disneyland,' she complained, 'while everyone else plays Goofy.'

The morning after the night before saw some of the men nursing gigantic hangovers, and raising a few eyebrows at what they mistakenly assumed the youngsters had been up to. Unable to face another day on the choppy sea, Vic announced that they would spend their second day playing crazy golf. Simon proved that he was better on dry land by winning the match, but appeared totally 'gobsmacked' when he was later presented with his winnings—not the money he had been expecting but a huge fish, packed in ice.

After a ride at the funfair, the merry band had had their fill of the seaside. And when they eventually piled into their minibus, more than happy to head homeward to Skelthwaite, only Dick looked sad. The delectable Cheryl, who had promised to wave him off, was nowhere to be seen.

As the bus turned the corner and drove away, Cheryl arrived outside the hotel—just too late.

THE MEN CLUB TOGETHER

When the men arrived back in Skelthwaite after their trip to Whitby, they were disappointed to discover that they had been unsuccessful in their bid for a grant from the National Lottery Fund to build a clubhouse for their local rugby team, the Skelthwaite Scorpions. Simon, who was still anxious to remain on good terms with everyone, therefore suggested that they themselves could raise the money needed to build it.

This seemed like a brilliant idea. As soon as Vic's plaster had been removed, he forged ahead with plans to get the building scheme off the ground. Fired up with enthusiasm after having been semi-infirm for so long, he hit upon the idea of staging a Festival of Mini-Rugby and Fête. Before long, the entire community of Skelthwaite seemed to have become involved in the preparations.

On the day, Henry caused a riot by dressing up as a scorpion, the Skelthwaite Brass Band provided the musical accompaniment to the revelries and everyone dug deep into their pockets, with the result that the event turned out to be a resounding success.

Vic and daughter Lucy enjoyed the revelries at the Festival of Mini-Rugby and Fête, organized to raise funds for the Skelthwaite Scorpions' clubhouse.

TRIP TO SEE SIGHTS PUT IN JEOPARDY

Bill Bowen, owner of the local hardware store, had been keen to help with the fête, so he sent son Nick backwards and forwards delivering wood and trestle tables. Nick was well known to Peggy because of the many eye operations he had undergone to repair his detached retinas. So she was alarmed when Vic accidentally knocked Nick's head with some wood as they went about their task of making preparations for the fête. She was aware that Nick's latest operation had been only four weeks ago and had a feeling that things were not going too well.

Earlier, Peggy had seen Nick at Skelthwaite Health Centre when he brought in his elder sister, Natalie, to have a septic pierced navel secretly treated by Peggy. He informed her that he was planning to spend a month travelling across Europe by train.

As Peggy dressed the cut on his head, Nick confided that he was having problems with his eye again—he asked her to promise that she would not tell his father in case he tried to cancel his trip. Peggy was torn between her loyalty to Nick and what she felt was right. After talking to Vic, she decided she had no choice but to speak to Bill about it. After all, she would have wanted to know if it had been Stephen in that position.

Bill was very upset when he heard of Nick's problems but he thanked Peggy for telling him. However, when Nick arrived home and discovered Peggy there, he felt betrayed. He lashed out, telling Peggy and his father that he wanted to see something of the world before he went completely blind. Then he stormed out.

Nick was in turmoil and went to the Skelthwaite Arms, where he inadvertently bumped into a man clutching a pint. Making no allowance for Nick's confused demeanour, the man rounded on him and pushed him roughly to the floor. Barely able to hold back the tears, Nick stumbled out of the pub and wandered into the night.

Meanwhile, Bill—who had raised two children single-handed since the death of his wife, Nancy—was beside himself with worry. When Nick failed to return home that night, he asked Peggy for help. While Natalie and Stephen searched the town, Bill and Peggy set out to look for Nick on the moors.

- Ironmonger Bill Bowen, father of blind Nick, was played by ROBERT PUGH, whose television roles have included gunman John Clarke in the 1985 *Brookside* siege, ambulance driver Ponting in *Casualty*, Handl in *Drovers' Gold* and Fr Matthew in *The Lakes*. Also a writer of stage plays, he acted in director Roman Polanski's film version of *Macbeth*.

Nick was later found, sitting on a wooden bench overlooking the town. He told Peggy that he knew his sight was deteriorating because he could no longer see the viaduct's 13 arches and he was cross with her for telling his father. 'It's scary to be ill,' he told Peggy. 'To keep control of it, you have to keep it to yourself.'

Bill told his son that he had a right to his own decisions and he would not cancel his trip if he really wanted to go. However, Nick realized that, with his eyesight deteriorating so rapidly, his father was right—he needed to go back to hospital for further treatment. The Bowen family were reunited at Nick's hospital bed after the teenager had been told that further surgery had only a one-in-three chance of being successful.

A REUNION FOR RUTH

Ruth began to mourn her lack of family. Her mother had moved to Australia after remarrying when Ruth was still in her teens, and letters sent to her grandmother, Nell, who lived in Harrogate, had remained unanswered.

The temptation to call in and introduce Alfie to his great-grandmother proved irresistible when Ruth found herself in the town with Jacqui, who was moving some of her belongings from her brother-in-law's house to Skelthwaite.

Ruth's heart pounded as she knocked on Nell's front door. Their introduction was awkward, but Nell invited in the two women in, together with Alfie. 'I've not come here to pick at old wounds,' Ruth declared when Nell began to malign her mother.

Going to Nell's kitchen to make cups of tea, Ruth and Jacqui were horrified to discover that it was in a disgusting state. It was obvious to them that the elderly woman was finding it difficult to cope on her own. The visit came to an abrupt end when Jacqui indelicately commented on the state of the kitchen. Nell was deeply offended and ushered the pair out of the house at once.

Nick Bowen (Stephen Graham) confided in Peggy as his sight deteriorated following operations to repair detached retinas, threatening his planned trip across Europe.

Ruth returned home dispirited, but she was determined not to give in, because she felt that Alfie had a right to know his great-grandmother. She made a further visit and the barriers began to be broken down. Nell explained that she had stopped visiting Ruth after being warned by Ruth's mother to keep away. She added that she did not care for Simon, 'a lad who peddled paper towels'.

Although Nell declined an offer to stay in Skelthwaite for a few days, Ruth was pleased that Alfie would now have something she herself never had—a real sense of family.

However, independent Nell eventually ended up at Ruth and Simon's home, after a nasty fall landed her in Harrogate Hospital, suffering from shock and with a badly bruised hip. Simon was furious, as he and Ruth had been due to fly to Tunisia the following day for a much-needed holiday in the sun. Now, instead of basking on the beach, they were stuck at home with 78-year-old Nell.

Nell was upset when she overheard Simon and Ruth arguing about their abandoned holiday. Simon stormed out, telling Ruth that he would have to go on his own. Nell was very distressed and said that she would rather be dead than a burden.

Vic, older and wiser than his hot-headed brother-in-law, managed to make Simon see the error of his selfish ways. He eventually apologized to Ruth, who insisted he did the same to Nell.

DICK'S DASTARDLY DEED

It was a day just like any other as Dick set off in a Goddard's paper factory van to Ashton-under-Lyne. He smiled widely as he told Vic, who had been relegated to office and despatch duties since his accident, that he was on his way to pick up a rugby 'scrum machine' that the team there were offering for free.

In high spirits, Dick sang 'Swing Low Sweet Chariot' as he headed out of Skelthwaite, calling a greeting to Peggy, who was looking for Lucy. But moments later Dick's world came crashing down around him as schoolboy Gary Kettle ran onto a new pedestrian crossing in front of him. Unaware of the crossing's existence, Dick failed to brake in time and hit the boy, knocking him unconscious.

• Kahil Kettle, brother of road accident victim Gary, was played by CHRIS BISSON, later to take the role of Vikram Desai in *Coronation Street*. He had previously appeared in *Children's Ward*, portrayed a drug-dealer's 'mule', who ended up dead, in *Prime Suspect 5: Errors of Judgement*, and worked as a presenter and director for Granada Television's Men and Motors channel. The actor can also be seen in a film version of *East Is East*, the West End stage play in which he appeared.

Gary Kettle's mother, June (Saskia Downes), was distraught when Dick ran her son over on a crossing.

Peggy ran across to help, relieved—she later admitted—that it hadn't been Lucy who was knocked down. Police and ambulance soon arrived at the scene and Gary, accompanied by his distraught mum June, was rushed to the hospital. Meanwhile Peggy took Dick, who was in deep shock, to the Health Centre to calm down.

Later, back at his flat, Dick was beside himself. When Vic and Terry came round to show their support, Dick asked why, if it wasn't his fault (he believed the new crossing should have been clearly marked), did he feel so guilty? Vic was firm in his view that it was a tragic accident and loyally stayed with Dick when the police arrived to tell him that Gary, a classmate of Lucy's, had died in hospital.

Skelthwaite was divided between those who supported Dick and those who believed he was at least partly to blame. On turning up for work, he was devastated to discover that Simon wanted him to stay at home until after the funeral. The paper factory boss also expressed concern that the incident reflected badly on his company, because Dick, as one of his employees, had been driving a works van. As a mark of respect for the dead boy, Simon closed the factory for the day.

Dick wandered aimlessly around and was drawn like a magnet to the iron railings near the accident, which had now become a shrine, covered in floral tributes and messages. He laid down his own flowers before going to the Skelthwaite Arms to drown his sorrows.

When he arrived at the pub, he was shocked when landlord Andy gave him a bottle of Scotch on the house but told him to drink it elsewhere. Dick was later charged with causing death by dangerous driving and escorted to the police station.

PEGGY'S CANCER SCARE

While Vic was happy to be out of plaster, and pleased that the plans for the clubhouse were nearing fruition, Peggy was miserable as she tucked herself up in bed. The nurse was terrified that she had ovarian cancer, the disease that had killed her mother when she and Simon were children. But Peggy kept these fears to herself, not wanting to worry Vic until she knew exactly what was wrong with her.

The following morning, Lucy became very upset when she saw her mother fall to the kitchen floor in agony. She ran to Ruth's house as fast as she could, but only Nell was in, so the girl asked Nell to pass on the message about Peggy.

But Nell did not do so until that evening. As soon as Ruth heard, she dashed round to the Snows' home, where Peggy bared her soul about her fears about having cancer. Ruth tried to be brave for her dearest friend and persuaded Peggy to make an appointment at the hospital.

THREE'S A CROWD

Ruth was angry with Nell for not passing on Lucy's message promptly and Nell's presence in the house was becoming increasingly irritating to her and Simon. The following day, the couple returned home to find Nell sitting with her coat on and her bags packed. But Ruth could not bear to see her grandmother hurt and told her that, although things had not been easy, they were still a family and should stick together.

Later, Nell started acting very suspiciously, going out in taxis in the morning and not returning until the evening. Ruth and Simon were at their wits' end, so Ruth decided they needed to tell Nell how they were feeling. Before they had the chance, however, Nell announced that she was leaving—she had sold her house in Harrogate and was moving into sheltered accommodation in Pine Tree House, Skelthwaite.

She had decided that Ruth and Simon needed their own space and she, too, wanted her independence. 'I need a place of my own,' she explained, as Simon and Ruth breathed a sigh of relief.

WORD GETS AROUND

Stephen was getting ready for his first proper date with Jacqui. Strapped for cash, he asked Henry—who had a job at the supermarket—for a £20 loan, pretending he wanted to put a sure bet on a horse. But Henry refused, telling Stephen that if it was such a certainty he would have a flutter himself. Eventually, Vic came to the rescue.

Stephen took Jacqui to a local Indian restaurant and quickly discovered the main drawback of living in a small town—the fact that everyone knows your business. To his embarrassment, the waiter turned out to be an old friend from school, who delighted in telling Jacqui that 'Snowflake' had been a 'love hound' in his younger days. What's more, the evening ended with Pat witnessing the pair kissing outside her front door.

To add insult to injury, Pat revealed this to Peggy, who was upset that Stephen had not told her about himself and Jacqui. In turn, Jacqui was upset when she discovered that Stephen had not told Peggy about them. So when he arrived to collect her the next evening, she failed to turn up for their date.

She could not be mad with him for long, however, and the pair were soon kissing passionately on the sofa at Pat's house, where

Jacqui's landlady caught them at it—to Stephen's horror. From then on, he insisted on kissing only outside the house. 'I used to call her Auntie Pat and she would buy me ice-creams,' he told Jacqui to explain his embarrassment.

New love walked into Stephen's life in the shapely form of recently qualified community nurse Jacqui Richards.

SON AND CARER ALL IN ONE

Peggy first came across Ben Bradley, another of her daughter Lucy's new classmates, when she attended the school's memorial service for Gary Kettle. Finding the boy loitering in the cloakroom, she hurried him into the hall. She learned from the headteacher later that Ben did not come to school often.

When Lucy came home with a watch that Ben had given her, Peggy felt she had no choice but to take the watch back to him and have a word with his mother. This was not to be. Peggy was alarmed to discover Ben and his younger sister Emily at home on their own (or so Ben claimed).

Peggy became suspicious, and, when she later spotted Ben going into his house with a carrier-bag full of groceries, at a time when he should have been at school, she decided a visit was called for. With Ruth at her side, she knocked at the door.

● Multiple sclerosis sufferer Sue Bradley was played by JULIA FORD, who acted Dr Liz Seymour in *Medics* and work-shop manager Annie Whitby in writer Lucy Gannon's prison series, *Insiders*.

Once inside, they found the children's mother, Sue, sitting in the front room. Her manner was prickly and extremely defensive. Her speech was so slurred that Peggy and Ruth concluded she must have been drinking. Sue told the nurses that Ben had been kept off school because he was unwell and that her husband was at work. The pair left, totally unconvinced by her story and sure that the family had problems.

Pretending that she had left her keys behind, Peggy later returned to the house together with Ruth. Sue realized that she did need help and now revealed to the nurses that she was suffering from multiple sclerosis. She also admitted that her husband had moved out when she suffered a relapse, but explained that she had tried to spare the children's feelings by telling them he had gone away to work on an oil rig.

Ben had been her rock. She could manage only the minimum of chores, so he had been doing all the cooking, cleaning and shopping, as well as caring for her daughter. She knew it wasn't fair on him. 'I want him to be a kid again,' she said, adding that she was afraid Social Services would take her children away if she went to them for help. Peggy reassured her that this would not be the case, but they could do various things to make her life easier—and provide someone to help with the cleaning, cooking and shopping.

DICK STRUGGLES WITH GUILT

Work had begun on the clubhouse! Simon had given the men time off work to get started on the task, and they were all eager to put their backs into it. When they stopped for a tea-break, Dick—still very depressed after the road accident—volunteered to go to the shop for a packet of biscuits.

Vic began to grow alarmed when Dick failed to return. When Simon appeared and reported that he had just seen Dick heading in the direction of the viaduct, alarm bells started to ring and Vic insisted they go and find him as quickly as possible.

But Dick was not about to commit suicide —he was on his way to visit June Kettle, the mother of the young boy he had run over. He knocked on the door and waited for her to answer. When she did so, it took her a while to realize who Dick was, but as soon as she did she sent Dick away with the harsh and unforgiving words: 'I don't want you turning up on my doorstep expecting me to make you feel better.'

Dick sat and sobbed at the side of the road and was discovered there by Peggy and Ruth out on their rounds. With Peggy's help, he managed to regain his composure and make his way back to the clubhouse, where the others found him on their return from the viaduct. Vic assured Dick that he had their full support.

STEPHEN SKATES ON THIN ICE

Stephen was brimming over with confidence. He felt his work at the special school was going well and planned an ice-skating trip to Bradford with three of the children: Darren, Paul and Kelly.

With Jacqui at the wheel of the minibus, they set off, passing Debs as they drove out of Skelthwaite. But, unbeknown to Stephen, some of the pupils had smuggled cans of beer into their bags. While he and Jacqui were having fun out on the ice, they got stuck into the alcohol.

By the time Stephen had noticed that the trio were not on the ice, it was too late— they were already running amok in the town centre. Unable to find them, Stephen had no option but to get in touch with the school. The headteacher was furious. On being told that the incident was the first of its kind in the entire history of the school, Stephen immediately feared for his future there.

When he eventually tracked down the drunken teenagers in an amusement arcade, he let rip at them with a stern lecture. His self-assured manner was torn to shreds, however, when the youngsters informed him that they didn't trust him. Even though he was in their own age-group and wore the same trainers, he was not one of them—he was still in charge. Stephen was so angry and wound up by this that Jacqui had to stop him from punching one of the sneering boys. Once back at the school, Stephen was relieved to find that he had not, after all, lost his job. But he was told to take the advice of more experienced teachers in future.

● JOSEPH JACOBS, later to play Tyrone Dobbs' friend Marcus Wrigley in *Coronation Street*, acted teenager Darren —one of the group of pupils from the Lord Harris School that Stephen Snow took ice-skating in Bradford.

Stephen was on course for a fall, enjoying himself with Jacqui while his charges headed for town armed with cans of beer.

PEGGY'S MOMENT OF TRUTH

It was the day of Peggy's test results. Both she and Ruth were trying to go about their daily routine as normally as possible, pushing their fears to the back of their minds. Then, at 4.30pm, Ruth accompanied Peggy to the hospital for the moment of truth. Ruth stayed in the waiting room while Peggy stepped nervously into the doctor's consulting room. To her great relief, she was told that everything was fine—she did not have ovarian cancer, like her mother, but fibroids.

Outside in the corridor, the two women hugged and Ruth broke down and wept. She had tried to be brave for Peggy's sake but had really been terribly afraid for her. She could not bear to lose Peggy.

At home, that night, Peggy told Vic what had happened and spoke of the frustration she felt at never being allowed to be ill herself. 'I'm not indestructible,' she said. 'Where do I go when I fall apart?' Vic hugged her and told her that he would always be there for her.

The Lake District was the beautiful setting for Peggy and Vic's silver-wedding anniversary treat, although they found the wrong cottage.

PEGGY AND VIC CELEBRATE

For his and Peggy's silver wedding anniversary, Vic wanted to take his wife of 25 years away for a treat, so he rented for a few days a waterside cottage in the Lake District that belonged to one of Simon's friends. Peggy was on edge, however, as they made their way along the narrow, winding roads towards their holiday destination. She found it hard to leave Skelthwaite behind because she was worried about Lucy and Stephen, despite Ruth assuring her that she would keep a firm eye on them.

After stopping off at a callbox to telephone home, Peggy at last began to relax, and she gasped with delight when Vic pulled up outside a romantic-looking cottage nestling at the side of a beautiful lake. Everything seemed rosy, and when Vic presented Peggy with a beribboned bottle of pale ale—the first drink he ever bought her—it was more perfect still.

That is, until Peggy carried out a check on the cottage and discovered that there were no beds or cooker—nor any heating. Despite this minor setback, they decided to stay, seeing it as chance to spend time alone with one another.

As they sat eating chips out of the paper, in front of a roaring log fire, they engaged in a deep conversation about who they were and where their lives were going. Vic pulled at Peggy's heartstrings when he told her how hurt he had been that she felt unable to tell him about her fear of having ovarian cancer. 'I thought we were a team,' he said, 'but you let me down. You never gave me the chance to help.'

Peggy admitted that she had been wrong to exclude Vic, and promised that she would never keep secrets from him again. 'You're the kindest, warmest and most loving man I've ever met,' she told him, following this up by demanding that her husband 'ravish' her then and there on the floor. Vic complied, in front of the fire. Afterwards, they huddled together before putting on their coats and going to sit, with a hot drink, outside on the verandah.

Although Peggy and Vic were enjoying their break, the couple did not relish sleeping in the cold on a hard floor, so instead they decided to go home early. On their return, however, they were met with two surprises —both of them delivered by Simon. Firstly, it turned out that they had been staying at the wrong cottage. The one belonging to his friend was 200 years old and had central heating and a jacuzzi.

Their second surprise came when Simon presented them with his anniversary gift— a magnificent goldfish pond, to say sorry to Peggy for killing her fish when he was a child. But this was no common-or-garden fishpond. Simon had hired a JCB and installed floodlights and an ornate fountain. Peggy gazed in admiration at her beautiful pond, until … BANG! Her little brother had done it again. The lighting short-circuited and the hapless fish were all electrocuted.

YOUNG LOVERS FOILED

With Peggy and Vic away in the Lake District, Stephen and Jacqui thought it would be the ideal opportunity for them to get to know each other a little more intimately. But with young Lucy in the house, not to mention a persistent aunt watching over them, nothing went according to plan.

When they arranged for Lucy to spend an afternoon watching videos round at her friend Katie's house, they were disturbed by Simon and his JCB in the back garden. And during their next would-be steamy session, Peggy and Vic arrived back much earlier than expected.

NEVER TOO OLD

While Peggy was away, Ruth and Pat were called upon to deal with one of their more unusual cases. 'Find out if she's completely mad or just extremely optimistic,' they were instructed by Dr Daniel Leeming, who had been asked for the mini-pill by 79-year-old patient Emily Parker.

Stifling their smirks, the two nurses called on the elderly woman. Emily lived in a grand house with her younger sister, spinster Grace, who was adamant that Emily did not have a 'boyfriend', adding that she was 'simple' and should be put in a home.

Ruth and Pat thought it had all been a mis-understanding when Emily remarked how silly she had felt asking for the contraceptive pill when she was much too old. But their relief was short-lived when she told them not to worry, she had made other arrangements —and held out a packet of condoms.

Wondering if Grace was right about her sister after all, the nurses organized for the Social Services to assess Emily, despite a plea for caution from Dr Leeming. However, that evening Ruth discovered that the old lady had been telling the truth all along, when she was introduced to Emily's elderly boyfriend, having come across the couple enjoying a drink at the pub.

WALTER WANDERS AND WONDERS

Walter Charlton arrived back in Skelthwaite after a place was found for him at the group home, but he was dismayed and confused to find that all the familiar faces seemed to have gone. The Snows were away, it was Cheryl who came to the door when he called at Dick's flat, and in addition he managed to anger pub landlord Andy when he called in at the Skelthwaite Arms.

George Cooper, the previous landlord, had always had a complimentary half-pint of lager waiting on the bar for Walter, but Andy was not familiar with this tradition and demanded 87p for the drink. This sent Walter scurrying out of the pub in alarm. He was no longer sure of himself in Skelthwaite now that everything seemed to have changed and he began to wonder if he would be better off back in Leeds.

Confused, Walter sat on the kerb until he was spotted by his old friend Ruth, who welcomed him home with a wide smile and a big hug. She took him round Skelthwaite to prove that nothing had changed all that much. As they entered the pub, which was full of the old familiar faces, Walter enjoyed a warm welcome while Ruth gave Andy the lowdown on the free drink tradition.

SUPPORT ARRIVES FOR DICK

Another Skelthwaite man on unfamiliar terri-tory was Dick, who was living a nightmare after the death of the child he had run over. Feeling no longer able to hold his head up in the local community, Dick decided to move on. He had packed his bags and was just get-ting ready to leave when Cheryl, the woman with whom he had shared a night of passion in Whitby, turned up on his doorstep.

Cheryl could hardly believe that this was the happy-go-lucky fellow she had taken such a shine to—Dick now seemed cold and unresponsive. When she pleaded with him to tell her what was wrong, he gave her a crumpled copy of the local paper, in which the accident was headline news.

Dick wept and, instead of leaving, Cheryl stayed on to support him. She told him that

she really liked him and that in time people would forget. Her openness won Dick round and he agreed to accompany her to the Skelthwaite Arms, where he was greeted warmly by his loyal friends.

Dick's new love, Cheryl (Kathryn Hunt), took him to the Skelthwaite Arms to help him face the world after the accident.

HENRY WINS DEB'S HEART

Another romance in the making was that between Henry and Deborah. He had always worshipped her from afar and was angry that Stephen seemed so insensitive to her feelings. But now that Stephen and Jacqui had become an item, Henry felt sufficiently confident to ask Debs out.

RIGHT: *After lusting after Deborah (Laura Crossley) for so long, Henry (Andrew Knott) was delighted when she agreed to go out with him.*

He was over the moon when she agreed to go for an Italian meal with him that evening, but things did not go quite to plan. She talked constantly about Stephen, remarking to Henry that the reason she had enjoyed the meal was that 'you and me can come out as mates and there's no funny business'.

Later, on her birthday, Debs invited all her friends to a party at the Skelthwaite Arms, where she sat drinking herself into a stupor as Jacqui and Stephen smooched on the dance

floor. Afterwards, Henry did the proper thing and walked Debs home, but declined her offer of a kiss because he did not want to take advantage of her when she was so drunk. She repaid him for his chivalry by vomiting all over the front of his jacket.

However, Henry's loyal devotion to Debs eventually paid off. Accepting that Stephen was now with Jacqui, she began to see Henry in a different light. When she spotted him gently untucking an elderly woman shopper's skirt from her knickers in the supermarket to spare her blushes, it brought it home to her just what a nice person Henry really was.

PROTECTION FROM THE TRUTH

When Edith Woodford was diagnosed with cancer and her husband Derek brought her home from hospital to die, Peggy was faced with a dilemma. Derek had led his wife to believe she had a year to live, instead of the few weeks the doctors were predicting. Peggy felt that Edith should be told the truth about her condition, whereas Derek wanted to protect her and argued that he knew her best. Peggy had no choice but to respect his wishes.

Edith's main goal for what was left of her life was to see her only son, Sam, who worked in the family car-repair business, happily married to his sweetheart, Vicki. However, unknown to Edith, Vicki had called the wedding off, telling Sam that she no longer loved him. The young man was devastated and bombarded her with declarations of love at the local super-market where she worked, in full view of the customers— including Peggy and Ruth.

A fracas ensued, during which Henry was knocked to the ground as he tried to remove Sam from the store. Peggy, realizing that something was desperately wrong, later visited Sam at the garage to talk to him. She said that his mother should be informed of his broken engagement—she had a right to know, and indeed would want to know. Peggy later put the same argument to Derek, spelling out the fact that he could not protect Edith from what was going to happen. No amount of optimism could prevent her from dying.

Meanwhile, Sam sought solace in the bottom of a beer glass at the Skelthwaite Arms. This resulted in a brawl when

● Derek Woodford, who concealed from wife Edith that she would be dead within weeks from her cancer, was played by DAVID BRADLEY, well known as Labour MP Eddie Wells in *Our Friends in the North*, drugs baron Alf in *Band of Gold*, Arnold Springer (Robson Green's father) in *Reckless* and Rogue Riderhood in the 1998 BBC adaptation of *Our Mutual Friend*.

KAYE WRAGG, notorious as Lucy Archer in *The Lakes*, checking out the area's most eligible men, played supermarket checkout girl Vicki, who broke off her engagement to Derek's car mechanic son, Sam.

a row between Dick and Sam escalated into a punch-up, in which many of the regulars became involved. Most of them were taken to the police station after landlord Andy panicked and phoned for help.

On their release, Sam made his way home, where Derek had already told Edith the truth. She comforted her much-loved son, who was far more important to her than any wedding ceremony—she just wanted him to be happy. Edith insisted that from then on she wanted to know everything, and asked to see Peggy and get a realistic assessment of her prognosis and treatment.

DANISH TEAM SAVE SIMON'S BACON

Ruth prepared an impressive buffet for Simon's prospective new customers from Denmark.

Business had been slack at Goddard's Paper Products for some time and the threat of closure hung constantly over the business. But a visit from potential Danish customers brought a glimmer of hope.

For weeks, Simon and Ruth practised welcoming their new customers in Danish and Ruth planned to lay on an impressive buffet on her day off from the Health Centre. Simon arranged for Skelthwaite's brass band to strike up a rousing tune as the visitors arrived, and all the workers, with a little help from Vic, were given a pep talk about creating the right impression.

Simon even found a job for Walter—sweeping up the waste paper from the factory floor. When Ruth pointed out that Walter would lose his benefits if he were to earn money, he readily agreed to the suggestion that he be paid in beer.

The visit ran like clockwork at first. The machines purred happily and Simon reeled off an impressive list of facts and figures about toilet and kitchen paper production for his guests. Then things began to go wrong, with Walter proving a real spanner in the works. When asked about his job,

Walter proudly revealed that he was paid in beer, much to the contempt of the Danish, who were even more shocked when Simon explained why.

Disaster struck as Simon tried to impress his Danish visitors at the factory.

The machines that had been running so faultlessly began to go haywire, sending toilet rolls whizzing through the air as Vic did his best to iron out the problems. But the greatest disaster of all occurred when a string of Danish and British flags, which Ruth had used to decorate the kitchen and buffet, fell onto the ignited gas ring and burst into flames. As the smoke grew thicker, the alarms sounded and the fire sprinklers burst into action, soaking everyone—including the visitors.

All seemed lost. Whatever could have gone wrong had gone wrong. But, while Simon licked his wounds at home, Vic was busy treating the Danish delegates to a typical Skelthwaite night out, complete with a few 'specials' from the bar. Things were going great—the Danes were having a good time and Vic was explaining how Simon worked. With the help of the alcohol, things began to warm up and the prospect of doing business did not seem such a bad one, which was welcome news for Simon when he arrived at the pub later that night.

But he could hardly believe it when a fight broke out between Dick and Sam Woodford. The evening's events began to mirror those of earlier in the day. But this time, instead of just getting a soaking, the Danes ended up in the clink with everyone else.

When they were all released, Simon—who by now could barely look his visitors in the eye—was amazed to find the Danish delegation laughing. They had not had so much fun in a very long time, they said, and they signed the contract on the spot.

VIC'S BLAST FROM THE PAST

Peggy and Ruth were at the home of Edward Smith, an elderly man in his seventies who had just been diagnosed as a diabetic. He was keen to administer his own insulin injections, but the nurses were not so sure about this.

Edward told them that he was looking forward to his daughter Angela's visit. She was flying over from her home in South Africa for the first time in years. As they left Edward's house, Peggy told Ruth that Angela had been one of her classmates and also Vic's first love. At the time, there had even been talk of wedding bells.

What Peggy did not know was that tall, beautiful and slim Angela had already arrived in Skelthwaite and had wasted no time in seeking out her old beau. She had discovered him with the rest of the Scorpions, putting the final touches to the clubhouse in preparation for the afternoon's opening ceremony, to be performed by the Mayor of Skelthwaite.

Vic was amazed to see Angela after 28 years. Although anxious about leaving his work, he agreed to walk her across the golf course to her father's house. The two spoke about their lives, their pasts and the present. Angela told Vic that most recently she had been living in Cape Town with her husband, who had now left her, and that she had no children.

- GEOFFREY BAYLDON, best known on television in the title role of the 'seventies children's series *Catweazle* and as the Crowman in *Worzel Gummidge*, played diabetic widower Edward Smith.

  His daughter, Angela, who had been Vic Snow's first love, was acted by CHARLOTTE CORNWELL. Charlotte first found fame as Anna in the 'seventies series *Rock Follies* and has more recently appeared in *The Men's Room* and in the Lynda La Plante prison drama *The Governor*.

FOLLOWING PAGES:
Peggy looked on as Vic danced with old flame Angela Smith.

As they approached the edge of the green, Vic insisted that he would have to return to the clubhouse and Angela was left to go on alone. Arriving at her father's house, she was shocked to discover that he had collapsed in the garden shed, and she immediately called Ruth and Peggy.

The two nurses were quite unprepared for Angela's hostility. Accusing them of neglecting her father and leaving him to look after himself, she threatened to report them and arrange for private nursing care instead. Ruth was furious, and Angela deeply embarrassed when she finally realized who Peggy was. Angela then confided in Peggy that her husband had left her for a younger woman, who was now pregnant with his child.

After so many years' absence, Angela and her father did some serious talking. She told him about her broken marriage and was moved by his reaction. She welcomed his support when he commented that it was nice to have someone else to worry about, not just himself. But Angela felt she no longer belonged in Skelthwaite—South Africa was her home now. She informed Peggy that she would be taking her father back there with her.

CLUBHOUSE CELEBRATIONS

Months of hard work over, a grand opening ceremony was planned for the Skelthwaite Scorpions' clubhouse. Hours beforehand, all hands were on deck trying to get things shipshape. Even the mayor chipped in when he arrived a little early, keen to get on with things as he had a dialysis machine to inaugurate in Huddersfield later that afternoon.

Spirits were running high, and when Kenny made a surprise reappearance, a big cheer went up. The burly New Zealander said that Lucy had phoned to tell him about the new clubhouse and he just had to come and see it. Peggy suddenly realized why her phone bill had been so high!

The stage was set. Everyone who should have been there was, and with the band playing and the bunting flying, it was a welcome finale for the men who had put in so much time and hard work. Skelthwaite had its own clubhouse at last! With a snip of his scissors, the mayor cut the red toilet-roll ribbon and pronounced the building open. A celebratory rugby match followed, with Kenny and Dick playing half a game each.

That evening, a dinner-dance was held in the church hall to complete the celebrations. Pat and Cheryl, who had worked hard all day preparing the hall, were well rewarded for their efforts by the sight of all the happy Skelthwaite folk turning out in their best clothes to party.

Romance seemed to be in the air. When Ruth insisted that Simon, who was DJ for the evening, turn down the volume and put on some slow numbers, things began to happen. Pat, who had long lusted after her former lodger Kenny, was to be seen entwined in a passionate embrace with him, Stephen and Jacqui were reunited and things even began to look promising for Henry and Deborah.

JACQUI'S SETBACK FOR STEPHEN

Stephen thought it would be a brilliant idea to go on holiday with Jacqui and was hurt to be told that she was already planning to go to Ibiza with her college friends and did not want him along. When he protested that he was her boyfriend, she knocked the wind out of his sails by declaring that he was nothing more than a friend and she did not

want to be tied down.

The pair rowed, then Jacqui talked things over with Henry, while Stephen found a shoulder to cry on, telling Debs that he had never meant to hurt her. But the argument was short-lived—Stephen and Jacqui were reunited at the clubhouse celebrations, thanks to a few wise words from Peggy.

CHERYL SAYS 'YES' TO DICK

Cheryl had stayed on in Skelthwaite with Dick and was beginning to think about finding a job in the town. She was thrilled for Dick when he was told that the charge he faced for the road accident was being downgraded to careless driving, because the new crossing had not been properly signposted. Instead of possible imprisonment, he now faced a £300 fine and points on his licence.

Cheryl knew that she wanted to stay in Skelthwaite with Dick, but was not sure whether he had the same feelings. When she told him that she planned to return to Whitby, she desperately wanted him to ask her to stay. Instead, he just walked away.

She later found Dick at the crossing, weeping. He told her that he owed it to young Gary Kettle to live the best life he could. He asked Cheryl to marry him and she accepted.

RIGHT: *Dick could look forward to a new beginning with the news that his charge was being reduced to careless driving and Cheryl's acceptance of his proposal of marriage.*

TONY HAYGARTH
as Vic Snow

Dependable Vic Snow not only supports his wife Peggy in her work as a district nurse but has a real sense of community. He brings many of the local menfolk together in the local rugby team, which he has both played for and coached. For Tony Haygarth, who plays Vic, *Where the Heart Is* highlights some of the values he himself holds dear.

'It brings back memories of my childhood in Liverpool in the 1950s,' says Tony. 'I can remember going next door to borrow a loaf of bread, and my grandmother sitting on the doorstep and talking to people as they went by. That's not make-believe now, either. In the villages in which we film, there are still old-fashioned values. But that's partly a Northern thing. It certainly doesn't happen in London.'

Tony was in the enviable position of being able to choose between four different jobs when he received the first script for *Where the Heart Is*. 'What I liked about it was the optimistic attitudes of the characters,' he recalls. 'Unlike in many soaps, people weren't arguing with each other all the time and there wasn't a predominance of sex and violence. It wasn't all negative. This was a nice, gentle family drama. People discussed things, rather than rowing about them. It was all about love and old-fashioned values, and was perfectly watchable for children.

'I have, in my time, played the odd villain and nasty character, but I really want to see more programmes like this. The fact that it attracted 12 million viewers and an audience share of more than 50 per cent proved that you don't need those kind of programmes to come up with a successful series.'

His role as a paper factory worker who is a pivotal part of the community also brought back to Tony memories of appearing on stage at the National Theatre in *Lark Rise to Candleford*. 'I really enjoyed that,' he says. 'I played the fruit-and-veg man, the pub landlord and Loony Joe, who had no words but was a great part.

'Everybody should be thinking more about community—world community. Watching Comic Relief, it makes me cry that we divorce ourselves, with all our wealth in this real greed and consumer society, from the poorer nations of the world. They're human beings like us, but with far greater problems, both financially and food-wise.

'I'm a Christian and I believe in all the values that go with that. Although I was born and brought up a Catholic, I was accepted into the Church of England in 1998 when my children were confirmed.'

Tony compares the character of Vic Snow to his father. 'My dad, who worked on the buses in Liverpool as a driver, an inspector and then a traffic controller, was a very benign, gentle man,' says the actor. 'He loved my mother. She could shout and go mad and do anything, but if I was arguing with her he'd say, "Don't argue with her. Let her have her say and she'll get over it." He was always the leveller and peacekeeper. Vic is very like that.

'I'm not quite as my dad was, although I think I'm getting more like him. Maybe it's playing Vic that's done that. But I've always had a lot of my mum in me. She was a bit erratic, a bit mad and argumentative!'

One thing that Tony does not share with Yorkshireman Vic is the character's love of rugby, having never played the game himself. But the Liverpool-born actor, who lives in Kent with his television producer wife Carole and teenaged daughters Katie and Becky, now considers himself an honorary Yorkshireman, having also worked in the area on the sitcom *Rosie*, one of the first episodes of *The Last of the Summer Wine* and series such as *The Wanderer* and *Farrington of the FO*.

In the 'seventies he played Compo's nephew in *The Last of the Summer Wine* and, over four series of *Rosie*, he took the role of PC Wilmot, best friend of Constable Penrose, alongside Paul Greenwood. Tony has also played other memorable television characters such as Frank in the Costa del Sol detective drama *El C.I.D.*, Mitch Maddox in *All Quiet on the Preston Front*, Bill Wilson in the first series of *Pie in the Sky* and Deputy Chief Constable Roy Johnson in *Our Friends in the North*. He has also had parts in films including *McVicar*, *A Private Function* and *Clockwise*.

Now, Tony's daughters might be following him into the profession. Both appeared in the second series of *Where the Heart Is*, as girls buying sweets in a shop, and Katie acted his on-screen daughter in the BBC series *Mr Wroe's Virgins*. Away from the camera, Tony—a keen poet from the age of 16—has been writing a book about the last decade of the Elizabethan period, which he hopes will find a publisher.

On screen, he still has a few ambitions left. 'I always seem to play supporting roles,' he observes. 'In my life, I've rarely been the star. I really would love to play the leading role in a film or TV series. I once acted Macbeth in a nine-month tour with the English Shakespeare Company. It was wonderful going on stage for two-and-a-half hours every night, knowing that you were only off it for about 15 minutes. It was very demanding, very taxing, but exactly the sort of thing I love.'

THOMAS CRAIG
as Simon Goddard

Self-made man Simon Goddard provides employment for many of the locals at his paper factory in Skelthwaite. However, actor Thomas Craig did not want to let the character become too showy and flamboyant. 'They wanted to put me in a Crombie and loads of jewellery,' he recalls, 'but I didn't want to go over the top and end up looking like Del Boy!'

However, the actor admits that Simon, whose slightly resentful brother-in-law, Vic, works for him, can sometimes feel a sense of self-importance. 'Simon's a reasonable enough bloke,' he explains, 'but he can get a bit above his station at times and think he's better than he actually is. He's the richest man in the village and doesn't mind everyone else knowing it.

'I rather think that he started out as quite a good salesman, made a little bit of money on the side and put it into his own business. He still drinks with the boys at the local pub, though, and he's the chairman of the local rugby club. It's just that he's single-mindedly business-orientated, so he would be good at making money.'

The chance to act alongside Pam Ferris and Sarah Lancashire, as his sister and wife respectively, came as a surprise to Sheffield-born Thomas, one of the few true Yorkshire-men in the cast. 'I went up to be auditioned for a part in one of the early episodes of the first series,' he says, 'but then I was called back and offered one of the main male leads. I thought then that, if Pam Ferris and Sarah Lancashire were in the series, it must be a pretty good job to land—and I was right! They're a terrific bunch to work with.'

Thomas was already known on television through his role as Ian McShane's sidekick, Berry, in the crime drama *Madson* and he followed the first series of *Where the Heart Is* by playing new squaddie Jacko Barton in *Soldier Soldier*. But the actor started his career with an apprenticeship to a Sheffield plumbing firm after leaving school at 16. 'It seemed like a sound job, and jobs were becoming very hard to get,' Thomas remembers. 'Then I started going to drama classes about twice a week as an outside interest, purely a hobby.

'I met this girl in a pub who was doing drama with a group in Sheffield. She was also a dancer and went off to be a Bluebell Girl in Paris. I fancied her, so I thought maybe I should get into these drama classes, if it meant meeting more girls like her!'

But Thomas's hobby turned into a career when he was made redundant from his plumbing job, after six years, and a former teacher advised him to apply to the Academy of Live and Recorded Arts in London, to train as an actor.

'The greatest leap of all was not changing trades but leaving Sheffield, where I'd been brought up and where my family still live,' recounts Thomas. 'In fact, I hated London

with a vengeance for the first six months and often thought of jacking the whole thing in. I was forever coming back up home—usually with a suitcase full of dirty laundry for my mother to do. But then I seemed to fit into things a bit better, it all fell into place and I haven't looked back since.

'I still keep in touch with all my old Sheffield mates, though. They're still friends and they now accept that I'm an actor. I think they thought that acting on stage was a bit poncey, but now that I've had a few breaks in television they reckon it's OK!'

One of those theatrical roles was at the West Yorkshire Playhouse in Leeds, where he played the married builder who beds his two teenage babysitters in the late Bradford writer Andrea Dunbar's raunchy *Rita, Sue and Bob Too*. Thomas's part was later taken over by *Boys from the Blackstuff* star George Costigan in the 'eighties film version of the play.

Thomas's television break came with a part in *The Paradise Club*, starring Leslie Grantham and Don Henderson, and he has also appeared in programmes such as *The Chief*, *El C.I.D.*, *Boon*, *Mr Wroe's Virgins*, *Peak Practice*, *Cadfael*, *Common as Muck* and *Prime Suspect: Inner Circles*, in which he played a detective alongside Helen Mirren. In between roles, however, he has had to go back to plumbing to earn money.

Since he now lives in London, returning to Yorkshire to film *Where the Heart Is* has made it easier for Thomas to follow the fortunes of Sheffield Wednesday, the football team he has always supported. But playing the game himself became more difficult as a result of filming schedules at the factory used as Goddard's Paper Products. 'We could only film at the factory at weekends when the real business was shut,' explains Thomas. 'I play football at weekends!'

JASON DONE
as Stephen Snow

When William Ash left after two series, Jason Done was given the daunting task of taking over the part of district nurse Peggy's teenage son Stephen Snow in *Where the Heart Is*—but he was completely unfazed.

'I hadn't been following the programme and I consciously decided not to watch anything with William in before I started work on it,' says Jason. 'But I was aware of the series, partly because I'd acted in *Wokenwell*, which was filmed in Marsden, one of the locations for *Where the Heart Is*.'

Jason came to the role at a time when Stephen had to grow up fast and face up to his responsibilities as an adult. He had previously ignored the overtures of fellow-teenager Deborah Alliss and had an affair with his English teacher, Wendy Atkins, before falling for new community nurse Jacqui Richards. Although the couple split up and he subsequently had a fling with another woman, Jacqui's announcement that she was expecting his baby led to her and Stephen getting back together.

'He had matured as a result of his involvement with Jacqui,' comments Jason. 'He also moved out of his parents' home. These were real life-changing events. But, from an actor's point of view, I hope the future isn't going to be all "happy ever after" for them. I like problems. In any case, it never is all sweetness and light, especially when you're young and trying to find your feet with a career while bringing up a young family. I hope we reflect the everyday problems faced by people in a similar position.'

Jason's acting ambitions emerged at the age of 14, after first wanting to be 'a pilot, a Boomtown Rat and a speedway rider'. On leaving school, he trained at the College of Performing Arts in his home city of Salford as well as gaining experience at the National Youth Theatre in London before making his television début in the 1995 BBC mini-series *Blood and Peaches*, alongside Rosemary Leach, Jeff Rawle, Roger Lloyd Pack and Jayne Ashbourne. 'I played Gary, one of four young people growing up in Bradford,' says Jason. 'It was about their aspirations and what the future held for working-class Northern folk.'

Next came the role of Brian Rainford in *Wokenwell*, in which Jason acted the youngest of three policemen working on a rural beat in West Yorkshire. His character was married to Fran (played by *Holby City* actress Nicola Stephenson) and the couple had a baby. 'I was the rookie cop, very content with his life, with no real ambition other than doing his job well and serving the local community,' explains Jason, who himself is single and lives in London. 'It's all very spooky because, like in *Where the Heart Is*, Brian's partner gave birth during the series—and it was filmed in the same area. I've been surrounded by enough kids now, without having any of my own!'

One of the most memorable experiences of Jason's career so far has been appearing as a wounded soldier on the train in the first scene of the highly acclaimed film *The English Patient*, shot in Tuscany, Italy. 'I got to kiss Juliette Binoche,' he says proudly. 'She'd just removed some shrapnel from my leg and I had to say, "You're the most beautiful woman I've ever seen—kiss me." And she did!'

Jason also went to Portugal to play an American army cadet in the Richard Harris film *Barber of Siberia*, set in 1805, but he stayed closer to home—in Wales and at Pinewood Studios—to film his role as King Arthur's illegitimate son Mordred in the epic mini-series *Merlin*, which has since been screened around the world.

Before joining *Where the Heart Is*, Jason recorded *The Passion*, writer Mick Ford's BBC mini-series about a group of villagers staging the Passion Plays, who, for the part of Jesus, employ a professional actor (played by former *EastEnders* heart-throb Paul Nicholls), who has an affair with Jason's screen mother (played by Gina McKee). 'I came back from university, dressed as one of the Roman soldiers and nailed him to the cross as part of the production,' explains Jason. But as Stephen Snow, his way of tackling problems has not been so drastic.

Away from *Where the Heart Is*, Jason has ambitions to do more film and stage work. 'Good theatre is exciting, but it's also very hard to come by,' he remarks. 'A couple of years ago I acted in the London première of a Sam Shepard play, *States of Shock*, which explored the darker side of the American Dream. It was being performed as part of a festival of Sam Shepard's plays at the Battersea Arts Centre, and he actually came over afterwards to meet those who had taken part. But I went on holiday and missed out on going for a curry with him!'

MARSHA THOMASON
as Jacqui Richards

The role of a caring district nurse in *Where the Heart Is* was a far cry from that of the 'sassy', beer-swilling footballer that gained Marsha Thomason recognition in *Playing the Field*. Soon, the demands of appearing in two successful series meant that the actress found herself switching back and forth between playing Shazza Pearce, in the BBC drama about life both on and off a women's football pitch, and Jacqui Richards in the more sedate fictional community of Skelthwaite.

'Jacqui was the same age as me, ambitious and stubborn,' says Marsha. 'She came into the town and ruffled a few feathers. Peggy and Ruth did things differently from how Jacqui had been trained. When she arrived she was amused that they didn't use computers, even though they had them sitting there. She's just very outspoken, but that upsets other people. Also, falling for Stephen —her boss's son—affected her relationship with Peggy.'

Greater responsibility in Jacqui's private life came with the realization that she was pregnant—after splitting up with Stephen, who, in the meantime, had an affair with the factory's strategy consultant, Alison Storey.

Independent Jacqui was determined that she would bring the baby up by herself, but she eventually agreed to go back to Stephen and the couple found a house to rent.

'Being pregnant meant that Jacqui had to grow up, and her agenda changed slightly,' comments Marsha. 'I know it was just a fling that Stephen had, but I can understand where Jacqui was coming from. I wouldn't be too happy if I was worried about being pregnant and my boyfriend had been having sex with another woman. If that was the sort of man he was, how could he be a good father?

'I'm into my career and so is Jacqui, so I tried to imagine what it would be like all of a sudden to find I was pregnant. It's a life-changing thing. She wasn't even in a stable relationship and it was a scary prospect.'

Marsha spent most of the third series wearing pregnancy padding. 'The first time I put it in, I went all maternal,' she recalls. 'I was asking people to help me up and so on.' When the time came to give birth on screen, Marsha prepared herself by watching childbirth videos and another of actress Lorraine Ashbourne, who gave birth in *Playing the Field* when she was six months pregnant in real life. 'I also asked my mother about the waters breaking, because I didn't know it could be painful,' says Marsha, who admits to having looked forward to the scene 'with trepidation'.

The Manchester-born actress trained at Oldham Theatre Workshop from the age of 12 and, three years later, landed a spot in the BBC1 Saturday-morning children's programme *The 8.15 from Manchester*, performing ten-minute dramas. 'They revolved around five schoolchildren facing a different dilemma each week,' she explains. 'Viewers had to phone in and say which way they would resolve it. It was good experience and

helped me to become more comfortable in front of the camera.'

Then, while studying for her A-levels, Marsha landed a role as a homeless junkie in the BBC 'ScreenPlay' *Safe*, featuring Kate Hardie, and a small part as a nurse saving the life of a gay Catholic clergyman in acclaimed writer Jimmy McGovern's film *Priest*. She also acted a heroin addict's daughter whose brother is murdered in *Prime Suspect 5: Errors of Judgement*, the last in the gritty series of Helen Mirren police dramas, but playing a stripper in the 1996 television play *Brazen Hussies*, starring Julie Walters and Robert Lindsay, was an unhappy experience. 'I didn't like it,' she says. 'There were loads of men in the audience, extras, who had to leer and jeer. That was horrid. I don't regret taking the role, but I hadn't thought about what it would be like to get up and perform in front of all these old men. I didn't take all my clothes off, but I felt very vulnerable. It's completely different from taking your clothes off for a scene with one other person.'

After abandoning a degree at Manchester University to play waitress Sally in the last series of *Pie in the Sky*, Manchester City soccer fan Marsha was cast as Sharon Pearce in *Playing the Field*, created by *Band of Gold* writer Kay Mellor. 'It's a wonderful ensemble cast,' recalls Marsha, 'although I didn't like football training at all because I hated having to get up early in the morning to run around after a ball. I completely understand the game and have followed it all my life, but when it comes to me playing, my feet don't do what my head's telling me! In fact, my younger sister Kristy plays my body double in *Playing the Field*.'

A double celebration was called for when, shortly afterwards, Marsha—who is single and lives in London—landed the role of Jacqui in *Where the Heart Is*.

MAGGIE WELLS
as Patricia Illingworth

Times have changed! That's something Maggie Wells soon discovered when she joined *Where the Heart Is*, as part-time district nurse Patricia Illingworth, when the series began. 'Most people have an image of the district nurse that goes back to the 'fifties, in which she's usually riding a bicycle,' Maggie observes. 'I had to get that stereotype out of my head. These days, they have computers and are highly trained. In an isolated community, it's lovely to know there's one on hand to visit you.

'It was good when the younger nurse, Jacqui Richards, joined in the second series. She had fresh ideas about the job, which caused a stir. She also moved in as Patricia's lodger, giving her a motherly role. It's cosy and nice to have the companionship.'

After having her heart broken by her former lodger, Maori rugby player Kenny, who returned to his native New Zealand, widow Patricia was glad to find new love with another of the rugby players, Gerry Flint. Arnie Hema, who played the part of Kenny, actually gave Maggie her first screen kiss, which might seem surprising in a career that spans three decades.

'I always wanted to be an actress,' remarks Maggie. 'I was absolutely determined, and trained at LAMDA from the age of 18. When I left, I found myself bouncing around from one job to another.'

She played Virginia in a 'Laurence Olivier Presents...' production of *Saturday, Sunday, Monday* and kitchenmaid Doris in three episodes of the still fondly remembered series *Upstairs, Downstairs*, set in a wealthy Edwardian household. She would have continued but had already accepted other roles.

'I spent most of my first five years working in television, because I'd given birth to my son, Christian,' explains Maggie, 'and it was easier than having to go away on tour.'

Maggie lives in Brighton with her husband, Carl Rigg, who played PC Frank Tyler in *Crossroads*, Dr Knight in *General Hospital* and NY Estates manager Richard Anstey in *Emmerdale* before turning to writing. He now has scripts for both *Emmerdale* and *EastEnders* under his belt.

Once Christian was five, Maggie switched to theatre, working for the first time with Pam Ferris in the touring company Shared Experience, and did little television work for ten years. Most of the stage plays in which she appeared were classical, including Simon Callow's Royal Shakespeare Company production of *Les Enfants du Paradis*.

When she returned to the screen it was in guest roles in programmes such as *Peak Practice*, as well as the feature films *Foreign Affairs* and *Fairy Tale: A True Story*.

After the second series of *Where the Heart Is* Maggie joined the company at the Globe Theatre, in London, to perform in *As You Like It* and *Mad World My Masters*, but appeared in only a preview performance of the second play after breaking an Achilles tendon during rehearsals. As a result, she had to return to her television role as Pat Illingworth with her leg in plaster.

Compensation came with a new on-screen love interest, Gerry Flint, played by Andrew Tansey. 'He's a bit of a bruiser,' Maggie comments. 'But since it didn't work out with the Maori, Patricia hadn't really had a chap since her husband, Alan, died. They're almost opposites, though, so it's a funny scenario.'

1998–9

Once *Where the Heart Is* had become firmly established as a Sunday evening favourite with television audiences, ITV commissioned 14 episodes of it for the series that was broadcast in the spring of 1999. For this third run a new producer, Avon Harpley, took over from Kate Anthony, who had left to join independent production company Tiger Aspect. In addition, creators Ashley Pharoah and Vicky Featherstone were no longer involved on a day-to-day basis.

Vicky returned to the theatre and Ashley continued as a consultant to the programme but wrote no episodes. 'I had told my stories and thought it was time to move on,' he explains. 'I was the last of the initial creative people left, so I was the final link to the first two series. The advice I gave the writers was to keep the mix of darkness and light, and not to go sentimental.'

One important on-screen change was the replacement of William Ash, as Stephen Snow, by Jason Done, who came fresh from making the international mini-series *Merlin* and the feature film *Barber of Siberia* with Richard Harris and Helena Bonham-Carter. Again, Stephen had a central role in the series, this time splitting up with girlfriend Jacqui, having a fling with the factory's new strategy consultant, Alison Storey, and then being confronted with the news of Jacqui's pregnancy.

'I wanted to send Stephen away to university for the second time but then bring him back once more,' says producer Avon Harpley. 'He simply can't leave Skelthwaite—it's his home—but I felt it was time for him to separate from his family. He moves out of his parents' house and into a caravan for a while, but it ends up with him living with Jacqui and their having a baby. Although Jacqui's prepared to bring the baby up on her own, we wanted to show that Stephen had been raised by his own parents with incredibly strong principles and wouldn't let any son of his grow up without his natural father.'

The patter of tiny feet was also on the horizon for Ruth, but a miscarriage caused her and Simon to drift apart and split up, in a long-running story that spanned the entire series. 'I wanted to see what it was that made Ruth stay with Simon,' says Avon. 'Out of that came the fact that, actually, it wasn't such a great relationship. I didn't want the classic situation of Simon having an affair. It's the small things that create the great gulf, the constant dripping-tap effect—all the things they don't do for one another. Having a miscarriage was a very emotional event for Ruth, and if it had been a really good, strong relationship, they should have been able to pull through together.'

However, the series started off on a happy note with Dick and Cheryl's wedding, which also served as a means of bringing the whole cast together and reintroducing them to viewers after nine months off the air. Henry Green's romance with Deborah Alliss also began to blossom, although he soon found himself being pushed rather too far, too quickly. 'The series highlighted the different stages of various couples' relationships,' explains Avon. 'Dick and Cheryl were held up as love's young dream, while other relationships were struggling.'

A major cast change for the third series saw Jason Done take over the role of Stephen Snow, which was previously played by William Ash.

Peggy showed another side to her character when she decided to enrol for Italian classes and go on a two-week residential course in Harrogate—the first time in 25 years that she and husband Vic had been apart for any length of time. Meanwhile, he faced the problem of his beloved rugby team dwindling as players left.

A new addition to the series was the Harrison family—Vic's sister Sandra, her husband Keith and their son Craig—who arrived in Skelthwaite from Bradford. 'To sustain a third series, I thought we needed to expand the community more,' says Avon. 'We didn't know much about Vic's background before, so we brought in a sister as somebody who would have worked with Peggy, as a nurse, years earlier. If you don't broaden the cast out, the series goes stale. But, in taking over as producer, I knew I had to keep up the humour, pathos and wit.'

The 14 episodes were filmed over eight-and-a-half months and scripted by eight writers. The cast outing this time was a trip by the men from the paper factory to the Lake District for a team-building course at an outward-bound centre. 'It's nice to see the regulars out of their normal environment,' says Avon. 'You can allow them to behave differently and let new heroes to come to the fore. Similarly, we set Episode 8 entirely at night to show everyone having a different experience. The night-time can be stunningly beautiful and magical, but it can also be quite frightening.'

One visual change which the new producer made to the series was to alter the opening title sequence. Avon added moving pictures of the leading characters to the photograph album-style stills to make it 'more dynamic', while making the filmed shots of fictional Skelthwaite less static.

The series proved to be a hit with viewers once again, even now that Ashley Pharoah had taken more of a back seat. This enabled him to write the BBC medical ethics series *Life Support* and a mini-series for Granada Television entitled *Anchor Me*, as well as to develop ideas for feature films. 'I really have to thank *Where the Heart Is* for all that,' Ashley remarks. 'I wouldn't like to leave the series completely —the characters are like real people to me now.'

DICK AND CHERYL'S BIG DAY

Dick and Cheryl's wedding day was imminent. All the arrangements had been made, with Vic as best man and Lucy as bridesmaid. All was running smoothly until, while on a shopping spree, Cheryl dropped the bombshell that she had been married before at the age of 18. Dick was shocked and jealous, and insisted on firing questions at Cheryl through a changing-room curtain as she tried on clothes.

Despite her reassurance that her short-lived marriage had meant nothing and that he was the man she really loved, Dick was unnerved by this news. But they kissed and made up, and Cheryl was determined that everything would be perfect this time round.

Her plans included a hen party with her friends on the night before the big day. The drink flowed freely as the women laughed and shared funny stories about their husbands and boyfriends. Peggy was a little put out, though, and had to bite her tongue, when she heard Stephen's girlfriend Jacqui announce that she did not intend to marry until she met a man who was 'bloody good and bloody ready'—the only trouble, she continued, was that 'they're scarce in this town.'

The following morning Cheryl was woken by Pat and Jacqui, who brought her breakfast in bed. But while she prepared herself for the wedding in a relaxed manner, things were rather more tense for Dick when Terry scorched the bridegroom's shirt with the iron.

When everyone eventually made it to the register office there was a delay, during which the lads escorted Dick to the pub to calm his nerves, while Pat, Jacqui and Deborah took Cheryl to the park to calm her down. Dick confessed to Vic that he was unsure whether he could go through with the wedding, but Vic pointed out that two lives had nearly been lost with the accidental death of Gary Kettle, and it was Cheryl who had pulled him through and given him his life back. Dick saw sense and the wedding went ahead.

Dick and Cheryl's friends in Skelthwaite joined them for their big day, marred only by Cheryl's revelation that she had been married before.

During the celebrations at the reception later on, Simon upset his wife, Ruth, by announcing her pregnancy in front of everyone. She dashed to the Ladies in tears, with Peggy hot on her heels. Ruth informed Peggy that the pregnancy had been unplanned, but added, not sounding very convinced, that it was just what she and Simon needed.

Back in the hall the wedding guests were all dancing, but Cheryl was bewildered to notice that people seemed to be laughing at her and Dick. What they could see but she could not was the iron-shaped burn on the back of his shirt when he removed his jacket to trip the light fantastic with his bride. As the couple settled down to married life, Cheryl found a job at a local estate agency.

THE BUSINESS OF DEATH

Ruth and her old schoolfriend Jenny Lyons went to collect Jenny's dying father, Ronnie, from hospital. The elderly man had cancer, but the doctors had told Ruth that the tumour appeared to be shrinking. They had also stopped his morphine because Ronnie told everyone that he was no longer in pain.

Jenny and her young son, David, had lived with Ronnie in his enormous stone house ever since the breakdown of her marriage to husband Kevin. She thought the world of her businessman father and told Ruth that he had been more like a 'dad' to David than his father himself.

Ronnie, who was only putting a brave face on his illness, led Jenny to believe that he was itching to get back to work. At the first opportunity he got dressed and went outside to watch his grandson practising kicking a rugby ball. His motto for David was: 'Remember, keep your eye on the ball and your heart on the goal.'

- Much re-shooting had to be done for the first episode of the 1999 series after new producer Avon Harpley decided that the original result was not quite right. Diagnosing script and casting problems, she had some scenes rewritten and drafted in veteran actor Peter Jeffrey and Judy Flynn to take over the roles of cancer sufferer Ronnie and his daughter, Jenny Lyons.

'Viewers had to believe the man was ill enough to be dying of cancer but robust enough to persuade his family that he was fine,' comments Avon. 'After watching the original, we felt the casting wasn't quite right and didn't portray what we needed. Peter and Judy came in and hit absolutely the right note. Episode 1 is always crucial and, if you get it wrong, you've lost it for the whole series.'

Peter's long career has included television roles in series such as *Elizabeth R*, *Lipstick on Your Collar* and *Middlemarch*, parts in films including *If...*, *The Odessa File* and *Midnight Express*, and stage appearances with the Royal Shakespeare Company.

Judy is best known on television for her roles as daft secretary Julie in six series of *The Brittas Empire* and Madge Althorpe in *The House of Eliott*. She also played a patient suffering from multiple sclerosis in *Peak Practice*.

When Peggy called round to see him later, Ronnie found himself able at last to let down his guard, after she confided in him about her own earlier cancer scare. He talked to her about his wife, Rose, who had died ten years before, and agreed with Peggy that the most frightening aspect of dying was the prospect of no longer being able to go on caring for your family.

Ronnie was delighted when Simon called round for some business advice—it felt good to be able to talk shop over a couple of cans of beer. Simon left pleased with Ronnie's suggestions that he should build his own storage space and learn to delegate.

Despite Ronnie's outward appearance, Ruth was convinced that he was in more pain than he was letting on. Yet, when she tried to talk to his daughter Jenny about it, the two friends ended up arguing. Jenny got upset and told Ruth that the doctors knew best and she was *not* a doctor. 'No,' agreed Ruth, 'but I know my job.'

Jenny was nevertheless disturbed by the thought that her father might still be in pain, so she decided to challenge him about it herself. At first Ronnie brushed the idea aside, but, when his daughter persisted, he finally confessed. Not only was he in pain, he admitted, but it was constant, and even worse at night. He knew that he was dying, he told Jenny. But he declared that he was now ready for it, and added that he thought it was time she and David prepared themselves, too.

Jenny patched things up with Ruth and conceded that her friend had been right all along. She told Ruth that she knew her father was going to die when she heard him calling out her mother's name. She realized he was closer to his wife—and to death—than he was to them and life. Ronnie passed away that night during his sleep.

VIC'S SISTER RETURNS

Peggy was amazed one day to discover Vic's sister, Sandra Harrison, and her son Craig waiting for her at Skelthwaite Health Centre when she returned from her rounds. Although pleased to see them, she suspected there was something that Sandra, who lived in Bradford, was not telling her. Peggy took her sister-in-law home with her, where they engaged in social niceties and small-talk. Sandra told Peggy she was planning to spend a few days with a 'mate', but Peggy was not convinced.

When Vic arrived, he soon found out the truth. His sister admitted that she had walked out on her husband, Keith. Sensing that she needed to talk, Peggy took Sandra to the Skelthwaite Arms, where she confided that the reason she had left Keith after 18 years of marriage was that she thought their son Craig, who had been in trouble at school in Bradford, would do far better in Skelthwaite. Skelthwaite was her home, she added, where her real friends were.

Peggy was suspicious when Vic's sister, Sandra (Melanie Kilburn), turned up in Skelthwaite with son Craig—after walking out on her husband, Keith, in Bradford.

Although he did not subscribe to this idea, Keith turned up the following morning with a caravan in tow. Peggy was bemused to see him carrying on as if nothing had happened, even giving her a Patsy Cline tape he had compiled. Vic was fuming, and champing at the bit to punch Keith, until Peggy calmed him down.

Sandra and Keith talked everything over in their car. She told her husband that she did not intend to go back to Bradford and that, if he wanted her, he would have to move to Skelthwaite. Keith agreed and asked Vic if they could park their caravan on his drive until they found somewhere to live.

WILL SIMON GET BITTEN?

As a result of his inspirational chat with Ronnie Lyons, Simon had big plans for his company, Goddard's Paper Products. Having decided to expand, he came up a with new marketing idea: 'Tiger Roll. The kitchen roll with detergent in it. The towel with bite.' Simon wasted no time in putting his plans into action. He took Henry Green on as a trainee manager and also hired glamorous blonde financial strategist Alison Storey.

STEPHEN FINDS COMFORT

True love seemed to have run its course for Stephen and Jacqui, and they decided to put an end to their romance. She was leaving Skelthwaite on a three-week course and he was due to return to university.

Although Stephen was sad that he and Jacqui had parted, it was not long before he was in the arms of another woman—Alison Storey. His hormones had gone into overdrive the moment he laid eyes on her, while

KAT GETS THE CREAM!
Strategy consultant Alison Storey wasted no time in making her mark at Goddard's Paper Products. She soon got the brush-off from Jacqui Richards after indulging in a brief fling with Stephen Snow, and her attempt at seducing Simon, after his split-up with Ruth, was another disaster.

'She came in as an outsider and was ostracized,' explains KATRINA LEVON, who played Alison. 'She found the people small-minded and latched on to Stephen partly to become accepted. I don't see her as a slapper—she just wanted to fit in. But when Jacqui got back with Stephen, Alison met with hostility all round.

'It can be horrible playing a role like that. Alison was really an innocent in the whole thing because she had no idea about there being another woman on the scene—in fact, there wasn't at the time of the fling.'

Katrina's career got off to a flying start when she left drama school early to take a role in Danny Boyle's Royal Shakespeare Company production of *The Last Days of Don Juan*. After further work with the RSC, she acted on stage at both the National Theatre and the Royal Court.

'My most enjoyable role was playing a tough, working-class Scouser in Judith Johnson's play *Somewhere*, at the National Theatre,' says Katrina. 'She was torn between a nice guy and a bastard. I was drawn towards the latter, played by John Hannah!'

Katrina's screen roles have included policewoman Gill Copson in *Backup* and parts in *Inspector Morse*, *A Touch of Frost* and *The Ruth Rendell Mysteries*.

In between stints filming her scenes for *Where the Heart Is*, Katrina did some research for a film she is hoping to make as part of her plans to branch out into production. Her sister, Jacquetta, is a make-up artist who worked on *Sharpe* and the films *Love Is the Devil* and *Rogue Trader*.

● MARTIN TROAKES, who previously played Sgt Bill Parkin in *Backup*, took the role of single parent Frank Turner. The actor has also appeared in *Tiger Bay*, *Dangerfield*, *Soldier, Soldier*, *Brookside* and *Sitting Pretty*.

---

he was still working at the paper factory. Jacqui had never been slow in coming forward, but Alison took his breath away when they spent the night together on their first 'date'.

Simon was furious about this relationship and stormed round to Peggy, telling his sister to straighten Stephen out and describing him as her 'tomcat in my back yard'. He also made work as difficult as possible for Stephen, telling him, 'You're too busy getting your leg over,' and declaring that Henry was worth ten of him.

In the light of Simon's reaction, and his own still raw feelings over the break-up with Jacqui, Stephen told Alison that he thought they should stop seeing one another. When he reported that Simon thought he was leading her astray, she replied that she had enjoyed it but would survive without him. The pair hugged and kissed goodbye, and Alison told him to 'get off to university'.

AMBITIONS KICKED INTO TOUCH?

Frank Turner was over the moon when his teenaged son Michael was selected for a trial at Halifax Rugby League Club. It was the answer to all his dreams. No more doing up dodgy cars, he told Michael, who worked in a garage—there was big money to be had in rugby.

Frank had brought Michael up single-handedly since the death of his wife, Mary, ten years earlier and he relied on Peggy for moral support. It was she who had encouraged him to get Michael involved with rugby in the first place. When Stephen bought himself a beat-up old Lada for £250, Michael, as a friend, agreed to get it working for him.

When out jogging one afternoon, Michael came across the Skelthwaite Scorpions training and decided to join in. Peggy and Frank looked on as Michael ran rings around Vic and the other players. But soon Vic had had enough so he tackled Michael, leaving him on the ground clutching his knee in agony. Vic felt terrible when he realized that this meant Michael would no longer be able to attend his rugby trial, and Frank was devastated at the thought of missing out on what he imagined could be a £6,000 signing-on fee.

After having his knee X-rayed, Michael continued to be hounded by Frank about becoming a professional rugby player. Eventually he snapped, telling his father that he was

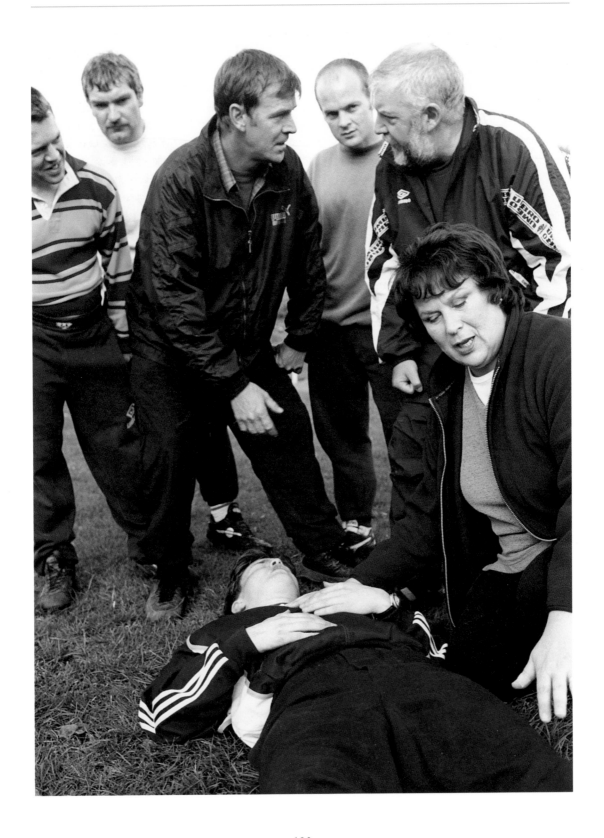

LEFT: *Peggy rushed to the scene when Michael Turner (Gerard Bentall) was felled by Vic's tackle on the rugby field.*

happy just as he was. He was not even sure that he wanted to play rugby. 'You're a sad, lonely man and everyone knows it,' he added. This was too much for Frank, who went berserk and punched his son to the ground.

Later, unable to find out where Michael was, Frank began to panic and enlisted the help of the Snows. They discovered him in the garage with Stephen's car. Peggy was shocked to see Michael's battered face and Frank said how sorry he was. She warned him to remember that, even though Michael was his son, they were two very different people.

Fortunately, Michael's injuries were not as serious as they had at first looked. But, when Frank went home, he started clearing all the trophies from the shelves on the living room walls—until Peggy stopped him, telling him that he didn't have to remove all their happy memories just because of one bad one. Father and son made their peace, with Frank declaring that he was ashamed of himself and promising that in future Michael could do whatever he wanted.

NURSES HOLD THEIR BREATH

- Feline-lover 'Cat Pee' Rita was acted by JEAN HEYWOOD, best remembered as Bella Seaton in *When the Boat Comes In*, Dolly Skilbeck's mother, Phyllis Acaster, in *Emmerdale*, Dolly McGregor in *The Brothers McGregor* and Aunt Dahlia in *Jeeves and Wooster*. She also played Sally Hart in the Channel 5 soap *Family Affairs*.

Ruth was scheduled to pay a routine visit to CPR, a woman known locally as 'Cat Pee' Rita because of the overwhelming aroma of cat urine that always seemed to surround her. The smell was so strong that the pungent whiff would announce her arrival before she even walked into a room. Despite this, Rita, who lived alone with dozens of cats, was a rather sweet old lady, but she was continually harassed by young hooligans throwing eggs and dirt at her windows.

She told Ruth that she was not feeling well, but when asked for a water sample she completely misunderstood and responded: 'Do you want it hot or cold?' When Rita arrived at the health centre later, clutching her sample in a large margarine tub, Ruth ticked Pat off crossly for making her distaste so obvious.

SNOWS HEAVY ON THE GROUND

With the Harrisons parked on their doorstep, life was rather overcrowded for the Snows. They were all beginning to get under one another's feet and Vic was being driven mad by having to queue for his own bathroom, particularly as he was not too keen on Keith.

Things were not much better in the caravan, as the three highly volatile Harrisons vied for space and Craig and his father bemoaned the fact they were living in Skelthwaite, calling it a dump. They both wanted to go back to Bradford. But the town was Sandra's home, and she was determined to muddle through as best she could until they could find a place of their own.

Helping Peggy out by taking Lucy shopping to buy her school uniform for the new term, Sandra astutely found one with plenty of growing room so that Peggy wouldn't have to buy another one too soon, and tailored it down with some deft needlework. Although things were difficult, everyone managed to make the best of the situation. Vic even amazed Peggy by telling her that he was getting on better with Keith. The best part of the day for Vic, however, was always when his sister and her family went back to the caravan for the night and he and Peggy were left alone in their house.

In searching for somewhere to live, Sandra and Keith scoured all the estate agencies in the area, but found mostly only modern boxes. Then Keith came across a derelict cottage

Keith Harrison (Neil McCaul) was enthusiastic when he found a property for conversion, but Sandra was not so sure.

with a barn attached, which was ripe for conversion and had a price he described as 'a snip'. He was brimming over with enthusiasm as he took Sandra to view the property, asserting that they both thrived on a challenge. Sandra was unsure about this, especially with the prospect of freezing in winter while the work was being done, but eventually she agreed.

BROTHERS IN ARMS

- Hypochondriac widower 'Fluey' Hughie Burridge was played by TONY MELODY, who had three roles in *Coronation Street* in the 'sixties, played ailing farmer Jed Outhwaite in *Emmerdale* in the 'nineties, and in between appeared in scores of programmes, including the sitcoms *Kindly Leave the Kerb*, *Down the Gate*, *Rule Britannia* and *The Nesbitts Are Coming*. He also acted in the BBC radio series *The Clitheroe Kid*.

   The part of Hughie's brother, Sam, was taken by another veteran actor, octogenarian PETER COPLEY, whose television roles, going as far back as 1938, have included Caesar in *Androcles and the Lion* and Abbot Heribert in *Cadfael*. Since 1934 he has also appeared in almost 50 films, including *Help!* and *Empire of the Sun*.

   The two actors previously worked together on television in *Moon and Son*, in which Peter played a colonel and Tony his batman.

Sam and Hughie Burridge were two warring brothers who had been arguing for years. While Sam had never married and appeared to have lived the life of a bold adventurer, including a spell fighting in the Spanish Civil War, Hughie had led a quieter life, settling down to marriage and his job for Leeds Corporation.

Hughie, a widower, was fond of going out for walks with Ruth's grandmother, Nell, who was now happily settled in Skelthwaite. The two of them spent an evening at a talk that Sam was giving at the village hall. The title of his lecture was the same as that of the book he had written and had published: *Letters from Catalonia, A Memoir from the Spanish Civil War*. While Nell sat transfixed, Hughie assumed an air of indifference—he had heard it all so many times before. With no regard for politeness, the brothers continually chipped away at one another. Hughie accused Sam of showing off about his time with the International Brigade, and Sam told Nell that they used to call his brother 'Fluey Hughie'.

When Hughie claimed he felt too 'worn out' for his regular walk with Nell, Sam jumped in and gallantly offered to accompany her in his place. But when Hughie heard this he decided to go after all, and the three of them embarked on a major trek across the moors, marshalled along by Sam.

On their return, the two brothers saw Nell home and then went back to Hughie's house, where they continued to bicker. Hughie told Sam that it was no wonder he was still on his own, since he never thought of anyone but himself. Sam stormed out but collapsed on the pavement, where he remained until Hughie spotted him later that night as he put out his rubbish.

The old man was rushed to hospital, where the doctors diagnosed that he had suffered a stroke. Refusing to leave his brother's side, Hughie maintained a constant bedside

Ruth's grandmother, Nell (Hazel Douglas), joined Hughie Burridge (Tony Melody) and his brother, Sam (Peter Copley), for a walk on the moors.

vigil, whiling away the time by reading Sam's book. When Sam regained consciousness, he was found to have some paralysis down his left side.

The two men talked. Hughie told Sam that he had always been his hero and confessed that he wished he, too, had done something as exciting as being involved in the Spanish Civil War. In return, Sam admitted that he had always viewed Hughie's stability and family life with some wistfulness. As the years of bitterness were put aside, the two at last became friends as well as brothers.

RUTH'S DEVASTATING NEWS

Ruth grew accustomed to the idea of being pregnant and began looking forward to giving birth to a baby brother or sister for Alfie. Simon, who was thrilled to bits, was convinced their child would be another boy. Despite putting in long hours at the factory, he was as supportive as he could be, making Ruth smile one morning when he told her, 'If I could have your morning sickness for you, I would.'

However, heartbreak came when Ruth suffered a miscarriage while at Nell's house. She later arrived at the health centre in tears and was taken home by Peggy. Simon rushed back from work and tried his best to cheer Ruth up by suggesting they book in for a long weekend in Ullswater while Nell looked after Alfie.

Struggling to come to terms with her loss, Ruth preferred to grieve alone and put on a brave smile for the world. But she found it too painful to talk to Simon, so excluded him. One night, instead of returning home, Ruth sloped off to the Skelthwaite Arms, where she found Vic and her other friends. She knocked back several gin-and-tonics in an attempt to deaden the pain, until Simon tracked her down, angry that she had not even phoned to say where she was.

Peggy and Simon were both worried about Ruth as she continued to distance herself

It was a shock for everyoner when Ruth miscarried and lost the baby that she and Simon had been expecting.

from them and refused to talk about the miscarriage. Needing young Alfie more than ever, Ruth kissed him and, with tears running silently down her face, lay down beside him after tucking him up for the night.

THE HAPPIEST DAYS OF THEIR LIVES

It was Lucy Snow and Craig Harrison's first day at Skelthwaite High School. Vic and Peggy's young daughter was a bag of nerves as she set off for the bus stop with her father. Vic reassured her that everything would be fine as she jumped aboard the bus with her Sean the Sheep rucksack strapped firmly to her back.

Apart from the slight sniggering that came from a bunch of older schoolgirls as she took her seat, all went well. It was clear that Lucy, as a first-year pupil, had no street cred with the older children, but that all changed, much to her delight, on the homeward journey. Instead of her father waiting to collect her from the bus, it was her good-looking big brother. The older girls gathered around the windows to get an 'eyeful' of Stephen, shouting out 'gorgeous' and 'sexy' at him. In return, he blew them all a kiss.

The following day, Lucy was a big hit with the other girls, who were keen to get to know her in the hope of having a chance to meet Stephen. Lucy lapped up all the attention and smugly told them that her brother would be collecting her again that evening, as he had promised. Her disappointment knew no bounds when she found Vic waiting for her instead. Lucy was so cross that she could barely bring herself to speak to her father, so the two of them marched home in silence.

Lucy gained street cred with her peers at Skelthwaite High School when brother Stephen met her from the bus to take her home.

But Lucy made a good start at the school, which was more than could be said for Craig, who frequently failed to turn up. When Sandra and Keith found out about this, they scotched his chances of sloping off again by delivering him to the doors of the school themselves.

'DRAGON' BREATHES FIRE

Elderly Kate Price had a reputation locally as being something of a dragon. She had lived at the same farm in Skelthwaite all her life and worked its extensive land until quite recently. But time had taken its toll and she was no longer a well woman. The fields had already been sold off and all she now owned was the large farmhouse, in which she rattled around all alone.

Now that, too, was to be sold and Kate would have to live with her son Roy and his wife, and their son, Eddie, in their home in Manchester. Roy arrived at the farm to help his mother prepare for the move, but he was shocked at her confused state, and bewildered to find her wandering barefoot around the farm, after dark, in her nightdress.

When Peggy called round to treat Kate for a minor ailment, she found the elderly woman 'a bit vague' despite her initially sharp tongue, which Peggy took in her stride. Roy told Peggy that his mother was terrified of ending up like her father, who in his later years had suffered from dementia. He wanted to know whether Kate had the same condition before moving her into his house, so Peggy agreed to consult her GP. Later that day, Kate flooded the kitchen by leaving a tap on.

When Peggy returned the next day to inform Roy that Kate was to be referred to a psycho-geriatrician for an expert diagnosis of her condition, he said he could not wait and would take his mother home with him the next day.

Then, when Eddie discovered that his grandmother was missing, Roy found her in the old stone barn that her father had built. Very confused, Kate mistook Eddie for Roy as a boy. Later, she told Roy that she could not leave the farm. When Peggy arrived the following day, Kate explained that she could not leave a place that so much work had gone into, adding that she had always promised herself she would die there.

Peggy felt that Kate might be suffering from depression, but Roy dismissed this and insisted that he would still be taking her back to Manchester with him. It was Kate herself who made Roy realize that she really did want to remain on the farm. Having no wish to go home with him, she offered Roy the money she had made from the sale of the land.

Mother and son talked, and Roy admitted that he wanted to take her to Manchester because he felt it was a way of

• CLARE KELLY, who played Kate Price, a widow living on a remote farm who was showing signs of dementia, is perhaps best remembered as Ken Barlow's first mother-in-law, Edith Tatlock, in *Coronation Street*. Her other roles have included Connie Wagstaffe in *The Cuckoo Waltz*, Mrs Braddock in *Open All Hours*, Joan Potter in *Crossroads*, a gypsy woman who put a curse on Amos Brearly in *Emmerdale* and Gwen Taylor's mother in *The Sharp End*.

Kate's son Roy was acted by DUNCAN BELL, who had previously played the part of Midshipman Clayton in ITV's *Hornblower* dramas.

allaying the guilt he had always felt about not taking on the farm himself. This was nonsense, his mother told him—he had no reason to feel like that, and she had always been very proud of him.

JACQUI DROPS A BOMBSHELL

Only days before he was due to leave for Bristol University, Stephen sent Jacqui a letter informing her of his fling with Alison. To his horror, he had only just posted it when Vic announced that Jacqui was due back that day.

Like a man possessed, Stephen raced back to the postbox, only to find that the mail had already been collected and was on its way to the sorting office in Huddersfield. In even more of a panic, Stephen admitted to Henry that he had planned for Jacqui to receive the letter after he had gone to university, so that he would not have to see her.

Dragonlike Kate Price (Clare Kelly) was determined to stay on her farm until her dying day.

Continuing his search for the potentially explosive letter, Stephen approached the local postman on his round and was pleased to find that he was an old classmate. But all hope of retrieving the letter quickly evaporated when he was reminded by his 'mate' that at school Stephen used to call him 'Pratt Man'.

In the meantime Jacqui was already back in Skelthwaite and, at the health centre office, had learned of Stephen's impending leaving party. Not one to give up easily, Stephen made for Pat's house and was invited into the living room to wait for Jacqui.

Having spied the offending letter, he tricked Pat into leaving him alone for a few seconds by pretending that he could smell gas. A bemused Pat, who used only electricity, went into the kitchen to investigate, giving Stephen just enough time to pop the letter into his pocket.

Within the next few moments, Jacqui arrived back before Stephen had the chance to beat a hasty retreat. It was then that Jacqui dropped the bombshell that she was eight weeks pregnant, at the same time insisting that she wanted to keep

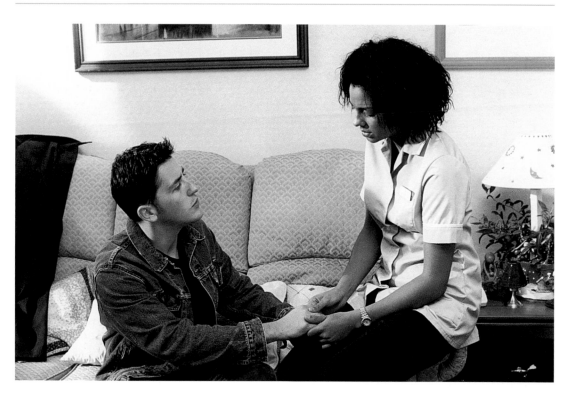

Stephen was relieved to recover the letter of confession he had written to Jacqui, but shocked to hear that she was pregnant.

the baby and bring it up in Skelthwaite. With Stephen still reeling from the impact of this news, Jacqui explained that she did not want him to abandon university—she intended to bring up the baby on her own.

Still in shock, Stephen left. He hardly felt in a party mood that night when Peggy and his friends threw a leaving bash for him at the Skelthwaite Arms. His mother noticed that something was wrong and followed him outside at the first opportunity to ask outright what was troubling him. Peggy wept as Stephen explained his predicament. Despite what Jacqui had said, he declared that he was not going to university. Peggy was both disappointed and worried about the financial implications they faced.

Meanwhile, at the health centre, Jacqui poured her heart out to Ruth, relating how angry and ashamed her parents had been when she told them of her pregnancy. Weeping, she recalled that as a child she had had so many big ideas, thinking she would set the world on fire, but in the end she was just the same as everyone else.

The next day, Peggy, annoyed that Ruth had heard about the pregnancy before she had, was told in no uncertain terms by Jacqui that she wanted to care for the baby single-handedly.

'I'm not stupid, Peggy,' Jacqui assured her. 'I know what's been going on. How can I think about raising a child with Stephen if he goes off gallivanting the minute my back's turned?'

Although he had been thrown into turmoil by Jacqui's decision, Stephen continued with his preparations to leave for university. However, he felt he could not go without seeing Jacqui once more. When she refused to come to the door at Pat's house, he followed her to the health centre, pleading with her to allow him to play a part in the baby's life. Jacqui told him that the best way to help her was to 'stop messing about, get your act together, get a degree and get some money'. Although she would love the baby, she added, she could not say the same about him.

So Stephen left for Bristol. But academic life had paled into insignificance now that he knew Jacqui was expecting his child. Although he did his best to settle down to his studies and get involved in the social scene, even the attentions of a willowy second-year psychology student failed to snap him out of his despair. Stephen had no time for her, or for her snooty friends who 'took the mickey' when he told them his father was a machine-minder.

Life at university seemed superficial to Stephen, and he soon realized that his heart belonged in Skelthwaite. Vic and Peggy were shocked when he arrived back home, but, more positively, Jacqui began to soften towards him. However, he was highly indignant when she told him there was a vacancy as a hospital porter. He did not get three A-levels just to end up as a porter, he declared.

When Stephen decided that it was time he left the family home, Peggy supported his decision to move into Keith and Sandra's now vacant caravan. His mother was sad that he was going, but Lucy was thrilled at the prospect of getting his bedroom at last.

Stephen was upset when Jacqui told him she'd been for her 12-week scan and showed him a photograph of the developing foetus. He again told her that it was important for him to be involved—he did not want to be pushed out.

JACQUI THE ACCUSED

Happy-go-lucky Alex Wrekin was confined to a wheelchair as a result of an accident three years earlier. His wife June had given up her full-time job as a legal secretary in Leeds to care for him. But when she sprained an ankle while lifting Alex into his chair, Peggy had to arrange nursing care while June recovered.

Social Services were unable to provide a care worker straight away, so Jacqui volunteered to step in. June continued with her secretarial job part-time and was pleased when Simon offered to pay her £200 cash for doing some typing—this would help the couple to afford a holiday in Majorca.

When Jacqui arrived to see her patient, Alex was in good spirits. The young nurse bathed him and helped him with his catheter, declining an offer of help from his wife. She chatted freely with Alex about Stephen and, when she needed towels, June told her that she would find them in the airing cupboard. After Jacqui's visit, June went to put the towels away and looked in the cashbox she kept in the airing cupboard. She was adamant that £200 was missing and phoned Peggy, accusing Jacqui of stealing the money.

Jacqui was devastated by this accusation, and by the fact that Alex believed it, when she thought they had got along so well. She felt alone and without allies—even Peggy seemed to be on their side. In fact, Peggy was worried that Jacqui might have been so scared about being pregnant that she had acted out of character. Peggy admitted to Ruth that she had not sent the official report that she was required to submit in circumstances such as these.

Jacqui got along so well with wheelchair-bound Alex Wrekin (Eamon Boland) that she was shocked to be accused of stealing from him and his wife.

Pat took over Alex's care from Jacqui, who felt by now that the whole world was against her. The young nurse started looking around for another job, even though, as she confided to Peggy, she had no desire to leave. Jacqui even admitted to Ruth that, because June seemed so convinced that the money had been stolen, she was beginning to wonder whether she was guilty after all but had somehow blocked it out of her mind. She was terrified that this could spell the end of her career and was thinking of giving the Wrekins £200 in an effort just to resolve the problem, despite the fact that this would seem like an admission of guilt.

But Peggy had a gut feeling that something was wrong in the Wrekin household, so she called round to speak to June. By virtue of revealing her own fears that Stephen might not need her any more, Peggy induced June to admit that she had not liked Jacqui taking Alex to the bathroom, as that had always been her responsibility. Eventually, June confessed to having taken the money herself. Peggy apologized to Jacqui and assured her she did not want her to leave.

- Wheelchair-bound Alex Wrekin was acted by EAMON BOLAND, whose numerous television roles have included Ken in *To Have and to Hold*, Clive in *Singles*, Gerry Hollis in *Kinsey*, Arthur Bryant in *Law and Disorder* and Graham Keegan in the parliamentary serial *Annie's Bar*, as well as two different parts in *Coronation Street*.

  SUSAN BROWN, who played Alex's wife, June, first found fame in the *Street* as dressmaker Connie Clayton. She has also been Helen in *Road*, Ruby in *Andy Capp*, Avril in *Making Out*, Jackie in *EastEnders*, Cilla in *September Song* and Maggie Belcher in *The Riff Raff Element*. In addition, Susan has worked with the Royal Shakespeare Company.

  In the same episode, Patricia Illingworth's neighbour, Mrs Webster, was acted by KATE LAYDEN, who had previously played Biff Fowler's mother, Sandra, in *Emmerdale*.

Alex later admitted that he, too, knew quite well that Jacqui had not stolen the money, but he had felt the need to back up June's story. The incident made the couple change their lifestyle, with Alex aiming to attend a workshop for the disabled and June planning to return to a full-time job in Leeds in order to earn more money. This would enable them to pay for extra help and get their lives back to normal.

SANDRA BACK ON COURSE

Ever since her return to Skelthwaite, Sandra Harrison had been determined to resume the career she had started when she trained as a nurse with sister-in-law Peggy 20 years earlier. The first rung on the ladder back to this goal was taking a job as a care worker. On Sandra's first day working at St Margaret's Nursing Home, Peggy called round to wish her well, bringing a card and an old photograph of the pair in their early nursing days.

Sandra took a job as a care worker as a means of getting back into nursing.

One of Sandra's first patients was 62-year-old George Brady, who was suffering from Huntington's disease. Finding herself drawn to his family, she badly wanted to help, as George's condition left him totally incapacitated. It was his birthday, and to celebrate it he was to be joined by his daughter, Jane, and his adopted son, Peter.

Jane arrived at the home in time to open the presents for her father, but Peter, who was flying in specially from Saudi Arabia, where he worked, arrived a little later, appearing tense and ill-at-ease. He had bought George, who was a music lover and used to be a keen musician, a sophisticated CD player so that he would be able to listen to his favourite classical music.

Later, when Peter and Jane talked together in the garden, Peter told his sister that he was to be married to Susannah, an engineer from Doncaster who was working with him out in Saudi. However, it was obvious from his manner that he was too embarrassed by George's condition to allow his father and his fiancée to meet.

Returning to George's room, Peter—who was paying the £600-a-week fees—was horrified to discover that Sandra, while busy in the other room, had nearly allowed her father to fall out of bed.

Peter tucked George safely back into bed before telling him of his impending marriage. He didn't know what to do when George burst into tears, but Sandra explained that an inability to control emotions was a symptom of his condition.

The birthday visit over, Peter returned to the family home and played George's piano. He was disturbed by a visit from Sandra, who had brought him a selection of leaflets on Huntington's disease and, unaware that he was adopted, gave him some information on coping with the risk of developing the condition himself. She also told Peter that, even though it might seem that Jane had everything under control, his father did want to see him.

Peter and Jane then opened up to one another. Peter admitted to his sister that he had felt excluded since the rest of the family had all gone to hospital for tests to see if they were carriers of the disease. He said he felt like an outsider, as if no one had any time for him.

Jane made Peter see that he was very important to them all, but particularly to their father, who had been looking forward for months to seeing him. She told Peter that he had fulfilled George's dream to have a son, and a musical one at that. In fact, he was their dad's favourite, she assured him.

AN APPOINTMENT FOR CRAIG

Starting work was not easy for Sandra. Her first day coincided with son Craig's visit to an educational psychologist, his form teacher having expressed concern that he might be suffering from dyslexia.

Administering a pep talk before he set off, Sandra was frustrated to see that Craig was more concerned about making arrangements to attend his friend Jamie's party in Bradford that night. He was put out when Sandra insisted that he could not go, as it was a school night and he was behind with his work.

On her return home that evening, Sandra was delighted to discover that Craig did not have dyslexia. She was touched when Keith presented her with a pair of gold earrings and a postcard from daughter Donna.

VIC AND PEGGY RING IN THE CHANGES

Vic was sad that none of the lads seemed to have their hearts in rugby any more when his team, the Skelthwaite Scorpions, lost a match against the Hoxton Giants because they had failed to scrape together a full team. But the Giants, too, were struggling to find enough players, so, taking up Stephen's idea of a merger, Vic arranged a meeting at the Hoxton Bell pub later that evening to discuss the idea.

Meanwhile, Peggy was absorbed in her Italian course in preparation for a planned holiday to Tuscany. Playing her tape and repeating the phrases while busy in the kitchen preparing a meal, she was looking forward to her first class. But then she remembered that Vic was also going out that evening, and they had no babysitter.

Peggy asked Craig, who had sat for them before, if he would look after Lucy until Stephen got home. The teenager obliged, but got annoyed when Lucy started teasing him about being in the 'special class' at school. He retaliated by telling her he had heard Peggy describe her as a 'pain in the neck'.

Peggy was the star pupil when Ruth accompanied her to her first Italian class.

This made Lucy cross with her mother, so she accepted Craig's suggestion that she go with him to his friend's party in Bradford. The pair made an ill-fated attempt to start Stephen's car, which they finished up reversing into the car behind. Giving up on this idea, they hitched a lift in a van.

Peggy sat through her Italian class blissfully unaware of all this, in company with Ruth, who had decided to tag along. Her hours of practice at home seemed to have paid off when the tutor described Peggy as her star pupil. Meanwhile, Vic's meeting with Gerry Flint of the Hoxton Giants was going from bad to worse, with both teams hurling insults at one another. They seemed to be incapable of putting the past behind them and building a joint future.

Peggy and Vic got home to find Sandra, Keith and Stephen waiting on the doorstep to impart the news that Craig and Lucy were missing. Although a frantic search followed, the youngsters' whereabouts became clear only when Craig called on the mobile phone. Keith and Vic went to collect the young runaways, who had not even made it to the party.

BEAUTY'S BEASTLY BEHAVIOUR

Young beautician Julie Cartland returned home after having major surgery to remove a large section of infected intestine. Instead of being thankful that she had survived, she was devastated to find she had been given an ileostomy.

Disgusted with having to use a bag, which was attached to a stoma, Julie refused to eat. She scraped the meals prepared for her by her mother, Pauline, into a tub concealed under her bed. She felt deeply ashamed and thought she had been disfigured. The final straw came when her boyfriend Matty, a chef, arrived to cook her a special meal. As he prepared the food, Pauline was surprised to discover that Matty had not been told the extent of Julie's illness and proceeded to explain about her daughter's colitis.

When Julie walked in on their conversation, she immediately assumed that Matty would no longer want to go out with her. She told him there was no point in their seeing one another any longer because they were obviously getting on each other's nerves.

Matty was heartbroken. That evening, as he mulled over his thoughts at the side of the canal, Keith Harrison arrived to do a spot of moonlight fishing after rowing with Sandra. Keith listened to Matty's tale of woe and did his best to provide a sympathetic ear.

Back at the Cartlands' home, Julie sobbed and admitted to her mother that she had really ended the relationship because of her ileostomy. She felt sure that Matty would not be able to deal with it and believed it was only a matter of time before he would walk out on her.

Pauline, worried that Julie did not seem to be recovering from her operation, called Peggy. The nurse immediately realized that Julie had not been eating and told her that the bag was essential to keep her alive. After a dressing-down from Peggy, Julie dried her eyes and agreed to stop being so silly. Peggy then took her down to the sheltered flats in Skelthwaite to work a little magic on Martha Bainbridge, who she knew would be delighted with a glamorous make-over.

Martha had told Peggy and Ruth on an earlier visit that her night of passion with boyfriend Albert had not been the 'hotbed of lust' that she had imagined, blaming this on Pat's efforts at hairdressing. She had advised the two nurses to take care of their minds and their faces, as her husband of 42 years

● Veteran actress HILARY MASON, who took the role of saucy pensioner Martha Bainbridge, has appeared in many films and television programmes. She portrayed one of two sinister sisters who befriended Julie Christie in the supernatural thriller *Don't Look Now* and Derek Wilton's mother in *Coronation Street*.

had left her after complaining that she didn't look after herself. But now Martha was thrilled with Julie's efforts, as were the other residents, who were falling over themselves to book a session with the beautician.

Julie thanked Peggy and then went to talk to Matty. He assured her that, although the ileostomy took some getting used to, he did not want their relationship to end after two-and-a-half years over something so trivial. He said that he loved her, and that was all Julie needed to know.

DAMP COURSE FOR THE LADS

Henry, who had now been going out with Deborah for months, was going from strength to strength in his position as Simon's trainee manager at the paper factory. When he suggested a team-building weekend at an outward-bound centre in the Lake District, the idea met with Simon's full approval, and the lads from the factory, along with Terry, were soon making their way across the hills in the rugby team's minibus.

But their hopes of spending a weekend away in a plush hotel were dashed when they found themselves having to bed down in Skelthwaite Scout tents. The men did their best to wrap up against the bitingly cold wind. And when Simon was introduced to the captain of the opposing team—Gareth Morgan, the toffee-nosed divisional head of Stonebrook and Gerrard Financial Services —it became obvious that the two teams were as different as chalk and cheese.

The opposition seemed able to sail over the difficult assault course with ease, while the Goddard team—with Henry as leader— lagged behind, totally unco-ordinated. The Skelthwaite men were seriously ribbed at the centre's bar later that evening, and then

had to return to their tents while the others went to a hotel. After a sing-song round a campfire, accompanied by Terry on the guitar, they settled down for the night.

Vic and Stephen devised a brilliant scam to give their team an advantage over their smug opponents. Stephen, passing himself off as the rival team's leader, asked the hotel reception to delay their wake-up call by an hour. However, the advantage was lost when Henry encountered problems with the map-reading and mistook the blue line indicating a river for a B-road, which resulted in the Skelthwaite crowd finding themselves confronted with a raging torrent of water.

When all seemed lost, the centre organizer turned up with a huge coil of rope and told them to get on with it. Henry was the first in the water, and would have been swept away

The men of Skelthwaite struggled to rise to the occasion when they went on a team-building weekend at a Lake District outward-bound centre.

but for Stephen's quick action in jumping in to save him. The others followed, clinging on to the rope, which had been suspended between two trees. Once safely across, they all breathed a sigh of relief and let up a cheer. After a short climb up a hill, they had made it home free.

But the team's celebration was short-lived. As Simon led the way to their goal, they discovered that the opposition, who had been fast asleep in bed when they set out earlier that morning, had beaten them to the finish line—using a footbridge over the river instead of wading through it!

JACQUI'S FOOD FOR THOUGHT

While the men were away, the Skelthwaite women decided to have a little celebration of their own in the form of a meal at the town's new Italian restaurant. The evening went well as the women became increasingly well oiled.

Peggy remarked to Ruth that the two-week residential Italian course in Harrogate for which she had enrolled might spur her on to do something with her life. But in fact Peggy was torn between wanting to attend the course for her own sake and worrying that the family would not manage without her. She and Vic had never been apart for so long. However, Vic later told her that he did not want her to feel guilty about going.

As the evening at the restaurant drew to an end, Alison Storey—bolstered by a glass or two of wine—sidled up to Jacqui and advised her to hang on to Stephen, saying he was special, 'one of the good guys'. 'If I were you,' she added, 'I wouldn't let him go.' This provided food for thought for Jacqui, who later slipped a note under Stephen's caravan door, inviting him along to her next scan appointment.

Relations appeared to be improving between Jacqui and Stephen, and he was thrilled when she accepted an invitation to go for a spin in his Lada. He took her on a magical mystery tour to a secret place that he had discovered years ago, when he was a Scout. As they chatted, Jacqui told Stephen that if the baby was a girl she was thinking of naming her Charlotte. He replied that he would have to try to think of a suitable boy's name.

On reaching their destination, Stephen led Jacqui across the moors, blindfolding her for the last part of the walk. 'This had better be good,' she warned him. And it was. Jacqui could hardly believe the beautiful sight that met her eyes—a secret lake. The pair climbed into a rowing boat and floated out into the middle of the water. As Jacqui lay back, gazing up at the stars, Stephen did his best impression of Leonardo DiCaprio in the film *Titanic*, shouting, 'I'm the king of the world,' before losing his balance and falling in, losing his car keys in the process.

Back on shore, Stephen stripped off his soaking wet trousers and tied a jumper round his waist to preserve his modesty, before he and Jacqui began walking home. Fortunately for them, Ruth, who was passing as she made her way to the hospital with a patient, stopped and offered them a lift. At the hospital, while they waited, Jacqui and Stephen kissed passionately in a corridor.

Jacqui eventually softened towards Stephen and allowed him to share in her pregnancy.

KEITH AND CRAIG GET SPOOKED

Sandra was worried that her husband Keith, who had decided there was money-making potential in the architectural salvage business, was not taking Craig's schooling seriously enough. Her concern was triggered by Keith's insistence on taking Craig out with him one evening to help him strip floor-boards for a mate, on the pretext that it was a good opportunity for some father-and-son bonding. They did not return home until the small hours.

Earlier that evening, as the pair arrived at the large stone building, which was being converted into a residential home, the door was answered by a stern-looking caretaker. The man seemed rather sinister, and all the more so when he informed them that his name was Bates. 'Not Norman?' quipped Keith. But his joke fell flat, as Bates—or Nobby, to use his first name—had never even heard of the film *Psycho*.

Keith and Craig got down to work and began industriously collecting all the loose boards. Some hours later, when they had nearly finished and were preparing to leave, Nobby related a chilling tale about a decapitated head wrapped in sacking that was said to have been hidden on the premises 50 years earlier. Craig's nerves were jangling like bells when he was sent back upstairs by Nobby to collect some more boards. Reaching over to pick them up, he spotted a spherical object bound in sacking. This was too much for young Craig and he cried out in alarm.

Keith and Nobby rushed upstairs, only to discover that it was just a ball. Keith was furious when he realized that the entire story had been Nobby's idea of a joke. His job was so boring, the caretaker explained, that it had given him something to do.

> ● Practical joker Mr Bates, caretaker at the building earmarked for development as a retirement home, was played by RICHARD MOORE, the actor who made audiences' flesh creep as kinky Curly in *Band of Gold* and took the role of Sir Paddy Penfold in *McCallum*.

SANDRA MAKES A SPLASH

Vic was rather enjoying Peggy's absence in Harrogate, having treated himself to a Chinese takeaway three times in a week. He was relaxing on the sofa, drinking a can of beer and watching *The Great Escape*, when his sister Sandra telephoned. Alone in the house while Keith and Craig were out stripping floorboards, she wanted Vic to go over and investigate a flapping noise that she had heard in the barn.

Once there, Vic discovered a bat. Sandra wanted him to finish it off, but Vic explained that bats were an endangered species. They left the doors open for the creature to make its escape and turned their attention to decorating Sandra's bedroom. The pair ended up working until 3.30am, emulsioning the walls a pale yellow.

When Keith and Craig finally returned home, they were amazed to find the bedroom finished—and Sandra and Vic fast asleep on the sofa.

A BABY FOR NURSE GODDARD

While Simon and Alison were busy number-crunching at his house one evening, Ruth was on night duty at the health centre. When she heard the sound of crying and went to investigate, she found that a tiny baby had been abandoned on the doorstep. Carrying the infant carefully inside, she unwrapped it and discovered a note that read: 'To Nurse Goddard.'

Ruth fussed over the baby, a boy, kissing him tenderly before finally phoning the local police, who were surprised she had waited two hours before contacting them. Before the child was taken away by the policewoman, Ruth asked for him to be called Joseph—the name she had chosen for her own lost baby.

Later, Ruth recognized local girl Paula peering through the health centre window. She went out to stop her and quizzed her about the baby, but only when she threatened to call the police did Paula own up that, although the baby was not hers, she had delivered it. The child belonged to her 16-year-old cousin Helen, who had arrived at her home only three days earlier. Ruth warned that it was vital for Helen to receive medical attention after the birth, and Paula agreed to take Ruth to see her.

They drove to a flat in Leeds and Paula waited in the car while Ruth went in to talk to Helen, who at first pretended that she was her sister, Sarah. The girl spun an elaborate web of lies, telling Ruth that Helen was away with their mother and father in London. She even faked a telephone conversation with her imaginary parents, but Ruth saw through the deception.

When Helen finally admitted her true identity, the two women began to talk. Ruth emphasized how important it was for Helen to accompany her to hospital. Her heart bled for the young girl as she was told of the hellish upbringing Helen had suffered. Her father had left home when she was only four, and her alcoholic mother had died six months ago.

Helen claimed she had not realized she was pregnant, as a result of a brief liaison with a 'bloke' she had met at a party. She said she had addressed the note that was

Finding an abandoned baby was a poignant moment for Ruth after her miscarriage.

• LOUISE ATKINS, who played pregnant prostitute Helen in the *Band of Gold* sequel *Gold* and the girlfriend of a man run over by a police car in *The Bill*, took the role of Paula, who delivered her cousin Helen's baby and left it on the doorstep of the health centre for Ruth to rescue. In her teens, the actress also played a 14-year-old gang leader in the television play *King Girl*. Helen was played by JULIA HAWORTH, who acted Miranda Pudsey in *3-7-11*, Sophie Burton in *My Dad's a Boring Nerd* and Lark Rothery in *The Grand*.

with the baby to Ruth because she had seen her with Simon and young Alfie, and they had all looked so happy together.

When the troubled teenager remarked on how lucky Ruth was, and how she seemed to have everything, the nurse told her of the miscarriage she had suffered only two months earlier. She added that her mother had left her when she was only 15, to go to Australia, and confessed that she felt she needed her mother now, more than ever before. When Helen explained that she had not even cuddled the baby, because there was no one to hold her, Ruth drove her to hospital to be reunited with her little boy.

SIMON MISJUDGES THE INDICATORS

Discussing business with Alison while Ruth was on night duty, Simon forgot to wake Alfie and give him his medicine. He was dismayed to discover that, even though profits at the factory were up and he had found an investor for his new Tiger Roll line, he had no money. He needed cash and the only way of getting it was to remortgage his house.

Simon and Alison then played cards and chatted together. Alison told Simon that she had taken a business studies course in America and admitted that, although she used to be romantically involved with someone, there was no one special now.

When Ruth got home after her traumatic night shift, she was upset and angry to find Simon clutching Alfie, who was obviously unwell. She took one look at her son, realized he had suffered a febrile convulsion and rushed him off to hospital. Tests showed that the boy had an infection. But despite having suffered a fit, Alfie was fine now and they were free to take him home.

However, the next day Ruth informed Pat and Jacqui that she intended to take some leave in order to look after Alfie.

VIC VICTORIOUS OVER MERGER

Vic carried on with his crusade to bring the Scorpions and the Giants together as a single Rugby League team by flyposting the whole of Skelthwaite with leaflets to bring attention to his cause. He wanted to make sure that everyone took part in the poll.

Dick was not planning to vote. He was against the plan for a merger, which he described as 'like mixing oil with water'. At the last minute, though, he had second thoughts, because Vic was his 'best mate' and needed his support. However, a flat car battery caused him to arrive just too late—the vote had already been taken.

Dick apologized profusely, thinking that Vic must have lost. He was therefore delighted when Vic announced that there had been a unanimous decision to merge the two neighbouring rugby clubs.

SANDRA'S DOUBTS PROVED WRONG

Former carpet fitter Tom Lewis, who now worked at Goddard's Paper Products, was married to Janet, a care worker at St Margaret's Nursing Home. The couple lived in a beautiful house that had previously belonged to Dr Braithwaite.

Tom's duties at the factory were not really to his liking, after his years spent travelling around different places fitting carpets, until his knees became too painful. He would arrive early at the factory, finish early, then take a nap in the warehouse before getting back on the job again. Henry was already unhappy with this situation, but felt he had no choice but to fire the man when it was found to be Tom's backpack and flask that had broken a machine after he fell into it.

Meanwhile, Janet had to rush to a patient's aid at the nursing home, when Sandra nearly caused the woman to drown by leaving her alone in the bath. Sandra felt dreadful about the incident, and began to worry that she might not be cut out to retrain as a nurse. Janet, a popular member of staff, calmed her down, stressing that it was purely an accident.

Janet's husband Tom wrongly suspected that his wife was having an affair with her close friend and colleague Bob Thorrold, but, on the contrary, Bob often gave Janet advice on how to revive her ailing marriage. Having been through a divorce himself, Bob strongly believed that talking was the key to survival and he urged Janet to talk to Tom about their problems.

That day, when Janet and Bob left work they agreed to meet up later at the Skelthwaite Arms. Sandra, waiting for a lift home from Keith, was amazed to find her husband reading Charles Dickens' *David Copperfield* to the elderly residents. She told him about the incident and then returned the books Jacqui had lent her to the health centre, explaining to her friend that she had decided against going back to nursing.

• Care worker Janet Lewis, working alongside Sandra Harrison in the nursing home, was acted by CAROLINE O'NEILL. As a teenager Caroline played sixth-former Andrea Clayton, who became pregnant by Terry Duckworth, in *Coronation Street*. She has also played policewomen in *Heartbeat*, the mini-series *Framed* and *The Lakes*, as well as taking the role of Margaret in *Men of the World*. GARRY COOPER, who was Supt Callard in *The Vice*, performed the part of Janet's husband, Tom.

Nurse Bob Thorrold, who Tom mistakenly thought was having an affair with his wife, was acted by WAYNE FOSKETT, best known as Keith in the series *Blind Men*.

Maggie, an old woman who nearly drowned when Sandra left her in the bath, was portrayed by ELIZABETH KELLY, who previously took the roles of Edie Burgess in *Coronation Street* and Nellie Ellis in *EastEnders*.

TOP: *Care worker Janet Lewis (Caroline O'Neill) turned to nurse Bob Thorrold (Wayne Foskett) for advice, to the anger of husband Tom (Garry Cooper).*

All went well at the Skelthwaite Arms until Tom turned up and tried to start a fight with Bob, who tried to reason with him. When Tom dashed out of the pub, Janet followed him to a park bench, where she began talking to him about their troubled marriage. Minutes later Sandra rushed up with Vic and, to everyone's amazement, laid Tom down and told Janet to call an ambulance. She had realized that Tom had suffered a heart attack.

Vic could not disguise his pride in his sister—she should definitely carry on with her nursing, he told her. When Tom recovered, he and Janet got talking and agreed that they did want to save their marriage. They were both prepared to give it another try.

Sandra embarked on her retraining course to go back into nursing. She was determined to do well, and burned the midnight oil to complete her 'homework'. She even became something of a star pupil, helping to demonstrate resuscitation techniques in front of the class and earning words of encouragement from her tutor.

MUSIC TEACHER OUT OF TUNE

Jacqui was pleased when Stephen informed her that he had landed a job as a teaching assistant at his old school, Skelthwaite High. And Stephen was happy to help out at the school concert that his inspirational music teacher, Martin Williams, had organized.

Peggy had dashed back after her Italian course in Harrogate to watch Lucy playing the triangle with great gusto. As refreshments were served after the performance, Martin took Peggy aside and asked if he could have a word with her some time that week.

That night, Martin and his teacher wife, Carol, strolled across the moor with their dog and talked about the success of the evening. But Martin appeared distracted. When they got back, Carol went to bed while her husband stayed downstairs. Soon afterwards, he went into the garden shed and, sadly, tried to commit suicide.

Martin was found unconscious by Carol the next morning and rushed to hospital in an ambulance. Peggy was on hand to comfort Carol, but she had taken the suicide bid badly and refused to go to the hospital, where her husband still lay

● Suicidal music teacher Martin Williams was played by TERENCE BEESLEY, whose many character roles on television include Derek Branning in *EastEnders*, four different parts in *The Bill* and others in *Campion*, *The Chief*, *Casualty* and *Cadfael*. ELIZABETH RIDER, seen as Sheila Thwaite in *The Lakes*, played Martin's wife, Carol.

Skelthwaite High School's headteacher was acted by DIANA DAVIES, whose list of memorable characters on television includes Doris in *A Family at War*, cornershop assistant Norma Ford in *Coronation Street* and both battered housewife Letty Brewer and Caroline Bates (mother of Kathy Glover) in *Emmerdale*. She also appeared alongside Glenda Jackson in the West End stage hit *Rose*.

In the same episode, Mrs Baker was played by PAULA JACOBS, who appeared in the films *She'll Be Wearing Pink Pyjamas* and *The Remains of the Day*, as well as playing Peggy Sagar in the television soap opera *Albion Market*.

unconscious. In a fury, she even smashed all Martin's picture frames with a clarinet, wondering what she had done wrong—she had thought that he loved her.

Stephen visited Martin, who told him that he had tried to kill himself because he felt his life was like being stuck in a lift that's forever going down. The future for Martin looked uncertain as he was collected from hospital by Peggy, wife Carol and their son, David. Stephen was devastated over the music teacher's suicide attempt, but Jacqui was on hand to comfort him. She put her arms around him and the two melted into a passionate kiss.

Music teacher Martin Williams (Terence Beesley) conducted a suicide attempt.

DEB'S DESIGNS ON HENRY

Deborah was putting pressure on boyfriend Henry for the two of them to become an item, like Jacqui and Stephen and Cheryl and Dick. In love with the idea of being in love, she wanted some kind of commitment from him. She cleverly manoeuvred Henry in the right direction by suggesting that they buy a plush flat together. Obviously none too keen, he made the excuse that her parents might not like them living together. But they would be happier, Debs reasoned, if she and Henry were engaged.

SIMON SNAPS—AND WALKS OUT

Simon was concerned that Ruth seemed to be showing no interest in returning to work. With all his current financial problems, he was anxious that her pay would be affected if she stayed off much longer. Ruth, on the other hand, was not worried about the money—she said she wanted Alfie to get to know his mother.

At the factory, Alison warned Simon that important invoices and major investors would need to be paid. If he delayed any more, the venture capitalists would start picking up what was owed by increasing their shareholding and soon they could have a controlling interest in the company.

Simon finally snapped when Ruth told him she wanted them to take Alfie away for a holiday in Fort William, Scotland, the following week. When he told her they couldn't afford it, a bitter row ensued, during which Simon confessed that he had remortgaged the house.

Ruth was very upset—her career was at a standstill, she was worried about Alfie, she had suffered a miscarriage, she didn't know what he was up to at work with Alison, and now, it seemed, they had no money. 'Sod off and go home to your factory!' she blurted out. Simon took her at her word and walked out.

Simon camped out in the paper factory, where Alison was only too willing to provide coffee and sympathy. But he was so perturbed that he was oblivious to her charms. Simon's priority was to work out a way to drag his business back from the brink. There would be no more Tiger Roll. 'Just plain toilet rolls for plain cash on delivery,' he told Henry.

When Ruth made it clear that she was not ready to return to work, a row followed and Simon left.

RUNAWAY SUCCESS ON SCHOOL CAMP

Spina bifida sufferer Tim Haynes had a reputation for being obnoxious and difficult. Stephen, as a classroom assistant at Skelthwaite High School, had to cope with Tim's wise-cracks as the teenager veered wildly around in his motor-ized wheelchair, hindering Craig and Stephen as they tried to prepare for a school camping trip. Stephen encouraged Tim to go on the camp, but he seemed determined to carry on wallowing in his problems. After all, he would be able to do nothing more than 'stay in and polish his crutches', he said.

Tim had no idea that his mother, Karen, was pregnant by her builder boyfriend, Geoff. She was deliberately keeping the news from her son until she had undergone a scan to check for spina bifida. Nurse Jacqui advised Karen that it would be better to break the news to her son sooner rather than later.

Geoff, concerned about the pregnancy, was giving Karen as much support as possible. He told her that he planned to take Tim to Elland Road football ground to see Leeds United play, as he had high hopes that this would put the boy in a good mood before they told him about the baby. But Karen delivered the news on the night before the match, and Tim took it badly.

The following day, as the schoolchildren boarded a mini-bus to set out for their camping trip, Tim told Stephen that he wanted to go after all, and that his mother would phone to give her permission later. Stephen folded Tim's wheelchair into the boot of his car before helping him in.

As Stephen, thoroughly fed up with Tim's cold, manipula-tive manner, helped him out of the car at the campsite, back at home Karen and Geoff were rowing over the boy. While Craig was getting stuck into his role as resident chef at the camp, teacher Anna Kelly began looking around for Tim, who had wandered off on his own. Despite his disability, Tim had managed to cover quite a distance on foot, moving deter-minedly along on his crutches. He finally made it to a large flat rock that looked out over the road, where he gazed defiantly out over the valley.

Jacqui, while being driven to the campsite by Stephen, was surprised when she spotted Tim up on the rock. The couple both tried to persuade him to return to the camp with them.

● MICHAEL JOWETT, the teenager who starred in the award-winning children's drama serial *Retrace*, played spina bifida sufferer Tim Haynes.

Tim's mother's boyfriend, Geoff, was portrayed by CHRISTOPHER WALKER, whose career has included a long list of roles: PC Nick Shaw in early series of *The Bill*, Brian Rimmer in *The Manageress*, Ray Thorpe in *Coronation Street*, Detective Chief Inspector Paul Boyd in *Our Friends in the North*, Lord Athelstone in *Ivanhoe*, corrupt footballer Bronco Layne in *The Fix*, Matthew Mullen in *Playing the Field* and Fred Stephens in *Sunny's Ears*.

When Tim refused, Stephen called the boy's bluff by driving off, but parking just over the brow of the hill, out of Tim's view. He remained on the scene while Jacqui went off to phone Tim's mother and tell her that he was safe.

Becoming increasingly concerned for the boy's safety, Stephen followed him as he set off through the undergrowth. When Tim eventually stopped, Stephen sat down beside him. The youngster wistfully recalled the good times he used to have there, when he and his father would share sandwiches and cream soda.

Tim began to mellow and cut the wise-cracks. Warming to Stephen now, he let down the barriers and spoke openly of the anxiety he felt about his mother's unborn child, and how he was worried that Geoff would make her 'get rid of it' if anything was found to be wrong with the baby. Tim seemed to take comfort when Stephen, in return, talked about Jacqui's pregnancy and admitted that he was 'frightened to death' by it all.

It was time to take Tim home and Stephen knew that he would soon have to face the music—he dreaded to think what trouble he would be in with the school. But at least he and Tim had come to an understanding, and the boy apologized to Stephen for conning him. Tim was welcomed home by his mother and Geoff, who were both relieved to have him back safe and sound.

Tim told them he was all right now and tried hard to understand as Karen explained the difficult situation. As they talked long and hard, he and Geoff even shared a joke about the football match they had missed.

Having returned to the camp, Stephen and Jacqui sat gazing up at the night sky. 'I love you, Jacqui,' Stephen told her, and she explained that she felt happy being both free and, in a way, trapped.

TORN OFF A STRIP

The merger between the Scorpions and the Giants rugby clubs got off to a bad start. Vic was worried that he would be held responsible, particularly when Gerry Flint arrived with the joint team's new shirts. The strip was dominated by the Giants' hated blue and purple hoops, with the Scorpions' green and gold present only on the collar.

At first, the Skelthwaite players refused to wear the new kit. But when Vic pointed out that a green and gold collar had been put onto the Giants' new set of shirts because this was the cheapest option, they finally relented.

The first day's training session got off to an even worse start when a Giants player known as 'The Butcher' stooped to wipe mud over the badge of the old Skelthwaite shirt he was wearing. All hell broke loose, with Vic and Gerry attempting to bring some short-lived order back to the game.

During the post-match drink, Terry and Gerry Flint resumed hostilities by arguing about an old plastering job that Gerry had poached. The pair ended up fighting outside, until Vic arrived to call a halt to the brawl. He told Gerry that they could not continue like this—and informed Terry that he had let the Scorpions down.

Nothing appeared to improve when Vic arranged a two-leg grudge match against Threlfall, a Rugby Union side. Playing Union rules in the first match, the Giant Scorpions lost 82–10. Afterwards, Gerry Flint challenged Vic over which of them should be the team's coach. Picking up a ball, he said that the first one of them to miss a conversion would lose.

Gerry converted with his first kick, but then Vic noticed that the ball was signed by 'sixties Wigan star Billy Boston, a big idol

of his. 'Tell you what,' suggested Vic. 'You let me have that ball and I'll let you coach the Giants.' A deal was struck, although Gerry later asked Vic to help him by motivating the team, saying: 'You get them ready for a battle and I'll show them how to win it.'

One person who was pleased to hear of Gerry's appointment as coach was nurse Pat, who admitted to Jacqui that she had been seeing Gerry. 'What is it with you and rugby players?' commented Jacqui. Later, Pat met Gerry's six-year-old daughter.

The rivalry continued between the Scorpions and the Giants even after the match, as Terry, surrounded by his team-mates, accused Gerry Flint of once having poached a plastering job from him.

SIMON DENIES AN AFFAIR...

Peggy was under pressure from the powers that be to find out when Ruth would be returning to work, but she felt awkward about probing, particularly when she knew how badly things were going for Ruth at the moment.

Shocked to discover that Ruth suspected Simon was having an affair with Alison Storey, Peggy decided to tackle her brother about the accusation. Simon strongly denied being involved in this way—with anyone—but he realized that it would not be a good idea for Alison to help him look for a flat. Deep down, he did not want to jeopardize his chances of a reunion with Ruth. Alison, well aware of this, appeared hurt by Simon's brush-off.

Simon's search for a flat ended with Cheryl taking him to view a property that was just right. But although it was what he wanted, he admitted that while he was still staying at the factory it was as if the split with Ruth were only temporary.

Meanwhile, even Ruth acknowledged that Simon was not having an affair. She told her grandmother, Nell, that she was just feeling sorry for herself. When Simon came home for a visit, Ruth and Nell thought a reconciliation might be on the cards, but he insisted on spending the entire visit upstairs with his son, Alfie. Nell tried to persuade her granddaughter to go up and speak to Simon, but Ruth decided she was tired of always being the one to make the first move. She was shocked, however, when Simon declined to stay for a cup of tea. 'No, thanks,' he replied curtly, 'I won't be stopping.'

Meanwhile, the nursing manager had issued Peggy with a letter to deliver to Ruth, which stated that she could have only two more days' leave.

...AND WORKS OVERTIME

The paper factory workers agreed to work at night to complete a huge order, without being paid overtime rates. There were plenty of yawns and red eyes, but Deborah appeared on the scene to cook enough food to feed a regiment, as the troops battled on in the hope of saving the factory.

However, Simon was nearing the end of his tether when an antiquated machine broke down the following morning, just as everyone reappeared, ready for a further attempt to meet the deadline. A new drive-shaft was needed, but because the part had to be sent over from Germany, it would not be possible to carry out the repair for at least another day.

Although he had found himself used and abused as a whipping boy during Simon's troubles, Henry proved his worth by coming up with the idea of all the workers forming a human conveyor belt and passing the goods along by hand, in order to complete the job on time and enable the venture capitalists who had invested in the factory to be repaid.

He followed this up with another master stroke—advising his boss to take payment for a foreign order in Deutschmarks instead of Sterling, because its value in the contract had been fixed against the Euro. This would enable the factory to gain ten per cent rather than lose that amount.

Once the shift was over, Alison congratulated Henry on his achievements that day. When the conversation turned to their boss, she asked Henry whether he thought Simon would go back to his wife. 'I'd say so,' was the reply. Disappointed at hearing this, Alison mentioned that her contract had only two weeks to run and said she would be sorry to leave. Realizing how she felt about Simon, Henry suggested she tell him.

FOR THE LOVE OF A DAUGHTER

When Walter returned to his boyhood home, with gardening tools in tow, he discovered a set of footprints in the flowerbeds, leading up to the house. After following the tracks, he peeped through a window and saw a tramp inside. Although he could hear the man talking, Walter was confused as to whether the man was actually speaking to anyone, as he seemed to be all alone.

Creeping carefully inside, Walter tripped over the tramp, who soon sent him sloping away by fixing him with a stern gaze as he continued his bizarre conversation. Walter was spooked by this, and got hold of the idea that the tramp must have been talking to a ghost.

Walter later returned accompanied by Peggy, who informed the tramp that he would not be able to stay there, but she said she could give him an address for sheltered accommodation. Taking out a pen and paper to write down the man's details, she was shocked to realize that he was Tom Palmer, an old friend of her father's. Peggy took the tramp back to the health centre, cleaned him up, dressed him in some of Vic's clothes, bandaged his feet, and dealt with his head lice.

It emerged that Tom had not spoken to his son-in-law, Joe Payne, since his daughter Maria had died. It came as a surprise when he heard from Peggy that Joe had remarried, and he remarked that there didn't seem any reason for him to stay. But Peggy insisted on phoning his son-in-law. As Joe and his wife Geraldine drove to the health centre to meet Tom, Joe confessed that he had thought his father-in-law was dead, claiming that he was a stranger to him now. Geraldine, however, believed that they should help the old man.

The couple arrived at the health centre while Peggy was taking Tom for a walk through the town. He was surprised to see all the council estates, and amazed when Peggy told him that the old mill had been converted into plush new flats.

When Tom returned from his walk, he was taken to Joe and Geraldine's house. Geraldine proposed that he should stay with them until the Social Services found him suitable accommodation, but Tom berated Joe for failing to tend Maria's grave, which he had found was 'overgrown with brambles'. Joe hit back by accusing Tom of neglecting to visit Maria when she was desperately ill.

When Peggy arrived she found Geraldine sitting on the doorstep looking pensive. Geraldine explained that she thought Joe had been keeping his feelings for first wife Maria bottled up inside. 'How can I compete with someone who's dead?' she asked. Joe joined the women outside for a while, but when the three of them went back into the living room they discovered that old Tom had disappeared.

Joe and Geraldine went to the graveyard where Maria was buried. Joe admitted that he still missed his first wife all the time, and the couple agreed to visit the grave together one day in every month. Tom, watching them from a distance, knew that his visit had paid off.

A GRAND HOUSEWARMING

Stephen and Jacqui proclaimed that they were moving into a rented cottage together and setting up home with their baby, and that the same evening they would be holding a house-warming party, to which everyone was invited.

Sandra also had something to celebrate. She had completed her last day as a care worker and would now be working as a qualified nurse alongside sister-in-law Peggy at the health centre. Before going to the housewarming, she shared a toast with Keith after he produced a bottle of champagne.

Simon, too, was clutching a bottle of champagne when he arrived at the party, but Stephen had to explain to his father, Vic, that he and Jacqui had really wanted to get everyone together so that they could announce their forthcoming marriage. Henry, however, got a shock when, at Deborah's instigation, Cheryl made another announcement—that he and Debs were engaged.

As everyone moved together for a dance, Simon plucked up the courage to ask Ruth to join him. The couple then walked around outside the house, and Ruth explained that she did not want them to split up, but longed for a fresh start well away from Skelthwaite. Simon asked her to give him until the end of the month to get the factory in order, pointing out that the lives of all his workers mattered too. At this, Ruth declared 'I'm not going to compete with half the town,' and walked back into the party. A reconciliation seemed unlikely after all.

When Simon collapsed at the factory, after the strain of successfully completing the company's huge order, Ruth and Peggy rushed round to tend to him. However, he had made sure that he was back at his desk by the time they entered his office, so Ruth left.

After Peggy had insisted that Simon go to the hospital and get checked over, he explained to her that he had wanted to show Ruth that he was strong and in control of things. But Peggy just told him to stop playing games and make a choice between his marriage and his work.

There were plenty of well-wishers when Jacqui moved into a rented cottage with Stephen.

A SETBACK FOR DICK AND CHERYL

Dick and Cheryl's hopes of starting a family appeared to have been thwarted when medical tests revealed that Dick had an abnormally low sperm count. He took the news badly, refusing offers of help from the hospital doctors, and was annoyed when Cheryl mentioned his problem to Peggy, pointing out that the nursing sister was married to his best friend.

Later, Peggy came across Dick in the graveyard, sitting next to Gary Kettle's headstone. 'How can I hold a baby in my arms, and watch it grow into the adult that this lad will never be?' he agonized. He didn't deserve children of his own, Dick added unhappily, but Peggy told him to let go of his guilt and get on with his life. Later, Cheryl was thrilled to hear that he had arranged an appointment at the hospital. They afterwards agreed to try the 'thermometers and calendars' method of conception and, if everything failed, to think about adoption.

HENRY PULLS BACK FROM THE BRINK

After the unplanned announcement that he and Deborah were engaged, Henry, the factory's trainee manager, began to feel that he was being pushed too far, too fast. Debs reminded him that they were about to sign on the dotted line for a house, and slipped in a mention of a three-piece suite she had seen.

Hours before the contracts were due to be exchanged on their house purchase, Henry confessed: 'I can't do it, Deborah. I can't marry you.' He explained that, although he loved her, he was not yet ready for marriage —or buying a house.

DEAF TO A CRY FOR HELP

Dick and Cheryl's neighbour, Faith Martin, was pregnant. Although both Faith and her husband Arthur were profoundly deaf, they hoped that their baby would have normal hearing. Faith's father, Gerald Webster, had not spoken to her for years, following a row, and refused to have anything to do with his grandchild's birth.

When Peggy told Faith that the hospital wanted Gerald to be a second contact during the pregnancy, she refused to agree. Cheryl volunteered to be one of Faith and Arthur's 'voices'—to talk to the baby, so that it could learn speech—but Peggy felt this should be done by someone closer to the family.

Peggy called round to see Gerald and urged him to help his daughter. At first just claiming grumpily that it was irresponsible for two deaf parents to have a child, eventually he accepted that he had blighted his daughter's life by only being able to think about her deafness. Later, he visited Faith and Arthur to make his peace and offer his assistance with the birth of their child.

> ● Deaf mum-to-be Faith Martin was played by ELIZABETH QUINN, a deaf actress who was acclaimed for her West End stage performance as Sarah Norman in *Children of a Lesser God*. ILAN DWEK, who acted Faith's husband, Arthur, is also deaf. This meant that a signer had to be on set when scenes featuring the pair were being filmed.

THE END FOR RUTH
AND SIMON?

When Ruth still failed to return to work at Skelthwaite Health Centre, Peggy had the delicate job of confronting her about it. If she continued to stay away, she would have to hand in her notice. But Ruth made it clear that she was not ready to return and had decided on her plans for the future.

Meanwhile, Simon's celebrations over the factory fulfilling its life-saving order were turned on their head when that company's boss, John Foster, phoned to tell Simon that he could not pay. This meant that the venture capitalists who had bought into Goddard's Paper Products would take control of the business. Alison insisted that she was to blame, as it was she who had put forward the idea of getting them to invest in the factory in the first place.

Simon put his arm round Alison to comfort her, and the pair kissed. But as she started to unbutton his shirt, Simon stopped her. 'I can't do this,' he declared. 'I love my wife.' Despite remonstrating with him, Alison realized that Simon had made up his mind, and decided to quit her job without completing the rest of her contract.

Meanwhile, Ruth was pressing on with her plans, helped by grandmother Nell, who presented her with the telephone number of her long-lost mother in Australia. Nell explained that Ruth's mother had always kept in touch with a friend over here so that she could find out what was happening in her daughter's life. Ruth called her mother, but afterwards, when she went to tell Nell the good news that she was to be reunited with her mum 'Down Under', Ruth discovered her grandmother lying dead on the floor next to Alfie's cot.

Later, Ruth received a letter from her mother, confirming the invitation for her and Alfie to go to Australia. When she asked Simon round to tell him that she intended to go, he was enthusiastic, remarking that her trip would 'clear the air'. And when she then asked him to move back into the family home while she went away, he saw it as a glimmer of hope for their marriage.

Meanwhile, at the factory, the venture capitalists' manager, John Morton arrived. Seeing how indispensable Vic was when it came to keeping the machines running, Morton gave him a letter with the offer of greater responsibility and more money. Vic put the envelope in his top pocket without opening it.

RIGHT: *Ruth finally burned her bridges with Skelthwaite—after suffering a miscarriage, splitting up with husband Simon and losing her grandmother, she looked forward to a new life in Australia with her long-lost mother.*

However, Simon still had a tenuous lifeline at Goddard's Paper Products. He told Vic that his principal backers, the Provident Society, were putting his shares in the business up for sale, but he had first refusal. If only he could get them back, between them he and the Provident would own a 51% majority share.

However, this one last chance of retaining control of his business seemed to slip from Simon's grasp when he found out that Morton had done a deal with John Foster. Simon realized that he had been stitched up. Without even having opened it, Vic later tore up the letter Morton had given him in front of his new boss. Henry speculated that the new régime would take the profitable new Tiger Roll from the factory and leave the other lines—maybe.

Simon's marriage seemed to be slipping from his grasp, too. Peggy, aware that Ruth would need money to go to Australia, handed her sister-in-law a cheque for £2,000—the money she and Vic had put aside for their holiday in Italy. 'I've never had this before,' said Ruth tearfully. 'My whole life, I've never had a friendship like this.' But Peggy was shocked to learn that Ruth had no intention of coming home again, and persuaded her to tell Simon the truth.

Meeting Simon, who was talking about joining her in Australia after a while, Ruth finally admitted that her mother had invited her to live out there permanently. Simon clung to the last hope he had for the survival of their marriage, insisting that Ruth simply needed time with her mother and stressing that he wanted her to be happy. But his wife replied: 'Simon, I don't know if I love you any more. I'm so sorry, but it's happened.'

On the night of her departure, Ruth bade an emotional farewell to Peggy, stepped into a taxi and left Skelthwaite, not sure if she would ever return.

JACQUI GIVES BIRTH

Jacqui's waters broke in the early hours of the morning on the day that Ruth left—just as Skelthwaite was subjected to a power cut. Stephen bundled her into his car and sped off towards the hospital, only for the vehicle to break down with gearbox problems. As he desperately tried to fix the problem, Jacqui warned him that she was close to giving birth. Luckily, he managed to effect a temporary repair using a length of wire.

At the hospital, Stephen was surprised to see his mother drive up, before Jacqui gave birth to a baby boy. Back at home later, the couple enjoyed visits from friends and relatives keen to see the new arrival, whom the couple named Jake.

THE MEN'S OWN FACTORY?

With Simon's shares in Goddard's Paper Products up for sale in two weeks' time, Vic hit on the idea of the workers themselves raising the £20,000 needed to buy them and thus regain control of the company, so as to save their jobs. Henry and Dick began taking pledges of money in the Skelthwaite Arms as Vic and Peggy mulled over Ruth's departure, the birth of Jacqui's baby and the now vacant nursing manager's job at the health centre.

RIGHT: *New life came to Skelthwaite in 1999 with the birth of Jacqui and Stephen's baby son, Jake, after a dramatic dash to hospital.*

WILLIAM TRAVIS
as Dick Lampard

Life has changed dramatically for paper factory worker and rugby player Dick Lampard. He has had to abandon his days of being footloose and fancy-free now that he's settled down with his new wife, Cheryl.

He has also been through the trauma of killing a child in a road accident, although in the end he was exonerated from blame, when it emerged that a new crossing had not been adequately signposted.

'Originally, I saw Dick as a bit of a wide boy, into his rugby and the "lad's" life,' says actor William Travis. 'He led the usual bachelor's existence, seeing his mates and drinking beer. But his life changed somewhat in the second series after he found the love of his life and was involved in a major accident that left him feeling enormous remorse. Cheryl brought him out of that deep depression and eventually he proposed to her, at the spot where the child died. He decided to dedicate his life to that boy.'

William, who is married with two children, claims that he was not a 'lad' himself. 'I was never one to sit in front of the telly with a few cans of beer,' he says. 'I was more likely to be out at a club dancing. But I did play rugby at school, so I've enjoyed that element of the programme.'

Having re-enacted Westerns in his back garden in Leigh, Lancashire when he was a child, William went on to train at the Welsh College of Music and Drama. By the time he left his wife Lorraine was pregnant with their daughter Elise, but the couple were homeless. 'We were living in a hostel near Wigan,' recalls William. 'Those were times you'd want to forget. I'd lost all my confidence—and lost my way.

'I went on the dole in between taking on jobs like telesales, or anything that would pay the bills. We really struggled for a few years. Eventually we got a council house in Leigh, back near our families, and through amateur dramatics I started to build up confidence again. My wife was wonderful and had a lot of faith in me. It really was a question of either pulling together or falling apart. But funnily enough, I think we were happy in our poverty.'

By the time stage work came along, at first with the touring Midsomer Actors company in *The Hound of the Baskervilles* and *As You Like It*, Lorraine had given birth to their second child, son Iwan. A Manchester theatrical agent then signed William and immediately sent him off to audition for *Where the Heart Is*. He had played a bit-part in *Emmerdale*, as a thug, five years before landing the role of Dick, and in between series he has played a gay-basher in *The Bill* as well as appearing in a *World in Action* programme about the exploitation of labour in the Third World.

KATHRYN HUNT
as Cheryl Lampard

Bubbly Cheryl Lampard swept husband-to-be Dick off his feet in Whitby, and then followed him back to Skelthwaite. 'It was an instant attraction and they both had a good time,' explains Kathryn Hunt, who played Cheryl. 'After Dick returned home, Cheryl had to decide, "Do I stay or do I go?" —and went looking for her man! That was proof of how much she felt for him.'

Kathryn enjoyed playing a strong female character. 'Cheryl used to run fishing trips in Whitby and she doesn't take any nonsense from anyone,' she observes. 'She's feisty and has a great lust for life. If she sees something she wants, she goes for it.'

Cheryl and Dick's wedding scenes were particularly happy ones to film, with the entire cast taking part. 'We really enjoy it when we're all together because we're like a family, we get on so well. I know it sounds corny, but it's true.'

Liverpool-born Kathryn had appeared in a string of television programmes, including *Cracker*, *Brookside* and the pilot of *Cold Feet*, before joining *Where the Heart Is*. her biggest break came as Irma, the housekeeper of Robson Green's father, in *Reckless*—appearing in both the original series and the sequel. She also acted Sarah Lancashire's best friend in the situation comedy *Bloomin' Marvellous*.

However, Kathryn turned to acting only in her mid-twenties, following experience as an insurance clerk, civil servant and bingo hall worker. After training at Manchester Polytechnic's School of Theatre, she failed to find work for 18 months. 'But I just kept going, bone-headed,' laughs Kathryn. Radio and theatre work eventually came along, and her favourite stage role was that of Paulina in *The Winter's Tale* at the Library Theatre, Manchester. 'A cracking part—and another strong woman,' she comments.

Between series of *Where the Heart Is*, Kathryn, who lives in West Yorkshire, played a small boy's nurse in the film *The Darkest Light*—a modern version of *Whistle Down the Wind* from the team who made *The Full Monty*. 'I'd like to do lots more drama,' says Kathryn, 'unless I achieve my ambition of becoming a catwalk model like Helena Christensen!'

LAURA CROSSLEY
as Deborah Alliss

Acting the role of Stephen Snow's lover in a school production of *A Streetcar Named Desire* was a gift for young Deborah Alliss, who was head-over-heels in love with the district nurse's son. So it was heartbreaking for poor Debs when Stephen launched into an affair with his English and drama teacher Wendy Atkins, and then fell for nurse Jacqui Richards.

'Debs was totally besotted with Stephen,' remarks Oldham-born actress Laura Crossley. 'She even got kissed by him, but he was only using her as a smokescreen to put people off the scent when he was seeing his teacher. Then, when he started going around with Jacqui, she thought that was bang out of order!'

Consolation came in the form of Stephen's friend, Henry Green, although Debs—by then babysitting Alfie Goddard by day and working behind the bar at the Skelthwaite Arms in the evenings—tried to move their relationship along too quickly. 'She realized how nice and how sensitive Henry was and wanted them to get engaged and move into a flat together,' explains Laura. 'She saw Dick and Cheryl getting married and Stephen and Jacqui setting up home, and felt left out.'

Laura had already played screen boyfriend Andrew Knott's sister in the film *The Secret Garden* when she was 12—an experience she will always remember. 'I had a scene with Maggie Smith in which she had to slap me across the face,' recalls Laura, 'and it was a real slap, not a stage one. We did three takes and my face and ear were bright red by the end!'

That role came five years after Laura started at Oldham Theatre Workshop, performing summer shows and pantomimes. At the age of nine, she had played the title role in *Chalkie* at Oldham Coliseum as well as taking a bit-part in *Coronation Street*. In her teens she played a drug addict in *Heartbeat* before concentrating on her GCSEs.

However, she abandoned her four A-levels when a London theatrical agent signed her up. She played Cindy Cunningham in *Hollyoaks*, a role that was taken over by Stephanie Waring when Laura left to play a girl who becomes pregnant, after being abused by her grandfather, in *A Touch of Frost*.

Laura was a pregnant schoolgirl again in *Bramwell*, portrayed a bully in *Casualty* and appeared in *Hetty Wainthropp Investigates* before joining *Where the Heart Is* at the age of 17. Since then, she has also acted 'a real tart who had to seduce her friend's trainspotter brother' in the Screen Two production *Anorak of Fire*. Another of the trainspotters was played by William Ash, the original actor in the part of Stephen in *Where the Heart Is*.

Titanic actress Kate Winslet has been Laura's greatest inspiration. 'She was around a long time before that film,' explains Laura, who is single and lives in Oldham. 'Once she was even in an episode of *Casualty*. That makes me think I'm in the same position now, doing the same sort of things—all I need is that one big break.'

ANDREW KNOTT
as Henry Green

Over three series of *Where the Heart Is* Andrew Knott's character, Henry Green, has been transformed from a schoolboy into a responsible trainee manager at Goddard Paper Products, complete with steady girlfriend. It seems a far cry from the role Andrew took in *Coronation Street* as Liam Shepherd, the no-good father of Zoë Tattersall's baby.

'I tried to make Henry a bit slow,' says Andrew. 'Not thick, but just not as quick to catch on as everyone else. That came from a scene where he was involved in a school show and the teacher kept shouting "Henry, the lights!". I thought he must be a bit dim not to register what she was saying.

'In fact, he turns out to be a bit of a bright spark in the end, because when the factory has a German contract agreed in Euros that's due to be paid in Sterling, it's Henry who comes up with the idea of accepting Deutschmarks instead, which gains the company an extra ten per cent after it's converted.'

Henry has also found himself a girlfriend —Deborah Alliss, who originally only had eyes for his friend Stephen. However, he backtracks a little after being catapaulted into getting engaged, telling Debs that he is not ready to make that commitment or set up home with her.

'Stephen was leading Deborah on all the way through the first series, and Henry was jealous,' comments Andrew, who joined the programme when he was 16. 'Then, on the trip to Whitby, Henry confronted Stephen, who told him to tell her how he felt. She had already seen that he was considerate and, at a party, he plucked up the courage and they kissed for the first time.'

Salford-born Andrew, who was brought up in Warrington, did modelling work as a child and then trained at Oldham Theatre Workshop, making his TV acting début as a child stealing Mavis Wilton's budgerigar in *Coronation Street*. Switching to films, he acted alongside Maggie Smith in *The Secret Garden* and Jim Carter in *Black Beauty*.

His other television roles have included that of a drug dealer in *The Ward*, a teenager stealing Jack Sugden's tractor in *Emmerdale* and the son of a murderer in *Cracker*. Andrew is single and lives in Wakefield.

MELANIE KILBURN
as Sandra Harrison

Vic Snow's younger sister, Sandra Harrison, aimed to start her life anew after 18 years of marriage by returning to her home town of Skelthwaite. Retraining as a nurse gave her an opportunity to take up the career she had abandoned when she married husband Keith, moved to Bradford and brought up son Craig and daughter Donna.

'Sandra is a modern woman,' says Melanie Kilburn, who plays the newly ambitious housewife. 'It's an incredibly brave thing for her to uproot herself, even though in effect she's going back home. Up until then, she had subjugated her life to her family. But she found a confidence that enabled her to go back and retrain.

'There are plenty of women out there who have done something similar, and hopefully even more will feel they can do it as a result of watching *Where the Heart Is*. There's still a lot of potential in Sandra.'

In the story the Harrisons bought and converted a derelict barn, but Melanie's memories of filming in the isolated real-life location, in the hills high above Slaithwaite, are not exactly happy ones. 'It was hell on Earth, and ghastly in winter,' she recalls. 'It was bitterly cold, smelly and horrible. Not the most comfortable of surroundings! Technically the place was difficult to film in, too, because the rooms were so small.'

Dewsbury-born Melanie, who was brought up in Bradford, began her performing career at the age of two, with Peggy Glenn's tap-dancing school in Batley. After training at a London drama school, she soon found work. 'My first job was as wardrobe mistress on tour with the New Shakespeare Company, which I'd joined as an assistant stage manager,' recounts Melanie. 'I shrank Calpernia's dress and irreparably creased Portia's!'

Melanie's first big role was as Jill in the BBC's Northern factory drama *Making Out*. 'That was terrific, written by Debbie Horsfield. It was the first of its kind, with strong roles for women,' she says. 'I look back on it with great affection and nostalgia.'

The actress, who is single and lives in London, also played a soldier's wife in the first series of *Soldier, Soldier*, Barbara Bibby in *The Lifeboat* and Charlotte in the comedy-drama *Moving Story* created by writer Jack Rosenthal, as well as a woman running an antenatal class in an episode of Sarah Lancashire's sitcom *Bloomin' Marvellous*. 'That was immensely nerve-racking, playing in front of a live audience,' recalls Melanie.

NEIL McCAUL
as Keith Harrison

Keith Harrison is the restless husband who followed his wife to Skelthwaite when their marriage seemed to be on the rocks. But actor Neil McCaul, who plays the Yorkshireman with an adolescent streak, did not know the fictional television town from Timbuktu before he landed the role.

'I'd never heard of *Where the Heart Is*,' confesses Neil. 'I hardly watch any television —I feel guilty if I do. And I certainly never watch daytime TV. But what I like about this programme is that it's given me a completely different character from normal. I usually get cast as probation officers or policemen—authority figures.'

Coventry-born Neil, who learned his craft in repertory theatres across Britain, has been unlucky enough to land parts in a string of West End stage flops. On television, he tends to be a bit-part player whose face is familiar to viewers, although his name is not even on the tips of their tongues.

'I've done a lot of parts in other people's series, such as *Class Act* and *Time After Time*, and played three roles in *The Bill* and two in *Casualty*,' says Neil, who is married with one daughter. 'But I've never really enjoyed television much until now. This is the first time I've had any length of time in which to find the character. Also, I now have this alter ego in Yorkshire. I stay in Huddersfield while filming and return to my family in London afterwards. It's a Jekyll-and-Hyde existence.

'I'm a great fan of Keith. He's one of those "can do" sort of people who get ideas and don't worry about anything. He lives spontaneously, for the moment. If he sees a tumbledown ruin of a barn, he just thinks: "We can live in that." Personally, I'd rather take my liver out with a wooden spoon!'

ALEX CARTER
as Craig Harrison

Teenage actor Alex Carter landed his first major television role when he joined *Where the Heart Is* as Craig Harrison for the programme's third series. 'Craig is dysfunctional,' says Alex. 'When his mother first took him to Skelthwaite, he just wanted to go home to Bradford. It wasn't until he saw a child psychologist that he realized his mum and dad were happy and started making friends. Maybe, as he gets older, he'll become less of a tearaway.'

Gelling with Melanie Kilburn and Neil McCaul as his screen parents was made easier for Alex by the nature of the story. 'They weren't all too close at the beginning,' he explains. 'That made it easier to build up the relationship.'

Born in Bolton and brought up in Saddleworth, Alex trained at the Ragged School in Manchester from the age of 12, made his television début in the Children's ITV series *Adam's Family Tree* and was then seen by millions in a Power Rangers commercial in which he was beamed up to a spaceship and told to save the world with a set of six-inch figures. Alex also starred in a BBC Radio 4 play, *Into the Dark*, with Sue Johnston in the role of his mother.

SIMON ASHLEY
as Terry *(on the left of the picture)*

Daydreaming rugby player Terry is a bachelor boy who has been left bemused by the fact that his friend Dick has married and no longer wants to spend all his spare time with his mates, swilling beer and watching television.

'Terry's very nice, but he's naïve and always misses the point,' says Simon Ashley, who has played the character since the programme began. 'He's developing into a kind of philosopher, who reads a lot of books but never learns anything from them!'

Simon landed the part of Terry after also auditioning as Dick. He had already played bit-parts in *Heartbeat, Coronation Street, Seaforth, The Last of the Summer Wine* and *Common As Muck*, but he started his show-business career as a comedian and singer in the Northern clubs.

'When I first left school, I went down the pit at Kellingley Colliery, near Pontefract,' recounts Simon. 'But after a couple of years I decided it wasn't for me and I became a scaffolder. In the evenings, I started doing "free-and-easies", the precursor to karaoke,

before getting an act together. I suddenly developed this ability to make people laugh and that's what led me into television.'

Acclaimed film director Ken Loach picked Simon to appear in commercials for *The Guardian* and Tetley bitter. He then started acting, and had his first major role in *The Merryhill Millionaires*, set during the miners' strike of the 'eighties. 'I was seen working on the coalface,' recalls Simon, 'and everyone was shocked when I told them I really used to work down the mines.'

This led to further television work, including the role of Stan in the last series of the comedy-drama *Common as Muck* written by William Ivory, who played Simon's sidekick in *The Merryhill Millionaires*.

'From that, I went on to *Where the Heart Is*,' says Simon. 'I was chuffed to bits. I still do comedy in the clubs and I'd like to do it on television, but there aren't any outlets now that *Opportunity Knocks* and *New Faces* have disappeared. My big ambition is to end up in musical theatre, perhaps in the West End.'

JESSICA BAGLOW
as Lucy Snow

Lucy Snow is part of a close-knit family. So much so that she even tried to stop her brother Stephen leaving home for university, by hijacking the letter containing his A-level results.

Jessica Baglow, the young actress who plays Lucy, is one of three children who have all acted on television—which is not surprising, considering that their mother runs a theatre school.

Jessica was born in Doncaster but now lives in Bolton. She had just turned eight when the first series of *Where the Heart Is* was broadcast, and soon found great support from her screen parents, Pam Ferris and Tony Haygarth.

'They help me a lot and give me hints,' says Jessica. 'I like Lucy because she's so exciting and adventurous. She's not afraid to do anything, like when she ran away with Craig, trying to get to a party in Bradford.

'One of my favourite scenes out of those I've appeared in was making bean-and-ham pie for Stephen. Lucy got beans, eggs and big chunks of ham and put them into a bowl and mixed it all up. I got it all over me and all over the place—and it smelled so bad. It was really fun!'

Since joining *Where the Heart Is*, Jessica—whose elder brothers, James and Richard, also act—has appeared in the Channel 5 legal drama *A Wing and a Prayer* with James. They played a brother and sister whose mother was trying to get her children back from their foster parents. Jessica's other brother, Richard, has acted in *The Ward* as well as appearing in an episode of *Verdict* featuring Sarah Lancashire as a barrister.

Jessica's mother, Denise, runs the Bolton Stagecoach Theatre Arts School. She trained as a lawyer but then switched to acting. Denise actually appeared as a barrister in *Verdict* herself, as well as a court welfare officer in *Coronation Street* and a jury foreman in *Emmerdale*. She even appeared as a woman on a bus in the third series of *Where the Heart Is*. Jessica's father, Neil, is a keen amateur actor who runs the Stagecoach school in Oldham.

'I want to be a professional actress when I grow up,' says Jessica, who particularly admires Mara Wilson, the young star of the film *Matilda*, which also featured Pam Ferris. 'She was scary in the film,' comments Jessica, 'but she's a really nice person in real life.'

GRAHAM TURNER
as Walter Charlton

Twenty-five years before landing the role of Walter Charlton in *Where the Heart Is*, actor Graham Turner was already familiar with the small towns where the programme is filmed. He used to work in the district as a van driver for Cadbury's. 'I delivered cakes in the area,' explains Wakefield-born Graham. 'In Slaithwaite, I used to go to the Co-op. When I started working on the programme, it was the first time I'd been back since 1972.'

Playing Walter, a man with learning difficulties, was a challenge to the actor, who had previously portrayed Edward 'Binny' Edwards in the prison series *Insiders*. 'I went to see a care worker who deals with people like him at a day centre,' explains Graham, 'but I wanted to respect the character, not do a caricature. I went for his childlike openness, and I was told that people like Walter like their routine and, if that goes awry, their world starts to crumble.

'He's an innocent—quite slow, the sort of person who always knows where to catch the bus but, if there are roadworks and he has to walk across the road, he can't deal with it. He's very much in the moment and doesn't look ahead too much. But everybody knows him in the village and looks out for him.'

In common with two other cast members, Graham turned up for the third series of *Where the Heart Is* in plaster, having snapped his Achilles tendon on stage in Wales. With Graham reliant on crutches, it was written into the script that Walter had tripped up on a rabbit warren while out on a walk with people from his sheltered accommodation.

Acting was always an interest for Graham as a child, but he took a 'sensible' office job after leaving school, before turning his hand to selling Cadbury's cakes, then Shredded Wheat. Seeing an advertisement in *The Stage* led him to audition for a role in Morecambe, where he made his professional début before working his way up to act with the Royal Shakespeare Company in productions including *A Midsummer Night's Dream*, *The Comedy of Errors* and *The Winter's Tale*. He has also acted in the West End in both *A Chorus Line* and *Hobson's Choice*.

A string of television roles followed, in programmes such as *Casualty*, *The Bill*, *A Touch of Frost* and *McCallum*. In addition there were his portrayals of a husband-beating victim in *Peak Practice* and a shopkeeper in the steamy drama *Close Relations*. 'I was the only one not to get my kit off,' comments Graham with a laugh.

Widely loved as *Where the Heart Is* character Walter, who always has his jacket covered with badges, the actor has been deluged with them. 'Kids, especially, love Walter,' says Graham, who lives in London with former *Peak Practice* and *EastEnders* actress Jacqueline Leonard, 'but I had a brilliant letter from New Zealand from the Billy Fury Fan Club asking if I'd wear one of their badges—so I did!'

INDEX